BUY ART SMART

BUY
ART
SMART

Foolproof strategies
for buying any
kind of art
with confidence

Alan S. Bamberger

Wallace-Homestead Book Company
Radnor, Pennsylvania

Published in Radnor, Pennsylvania 19089, by Wallace-Homestead,
a division of Chilton Book Company

Designed by Anthony Jacobson
Manufactured in the United States of America

Library of Congress Cataloging in Publication Data
Bamberger, Alan S.
    Buy art smart: foolproof strategies for buying any kind of art with confidence /
Alan S. Bamberger.
        p.   cm.
    Includes index.
    ISBN 0-87069-530-4 (pb)
    1. Art—Collectors and collecting.   I. Title.
    N5200.B36   1990   89-51553
707'.5—dc20   CIP

1 2 3 4 5 6 7 8 9 0   9 8 7 6 5 4 3 2 1 0

Contents

Acknowledgments   ix

Introduction   1

Part I: Identify 3

Chapter 1: What This Book Is About   5
    Facts about This Book 5
    The Four Steps to Buying Art Smart 7

Chapter 2: Discovering What You Like   11
    Look, Look, Look 12
    How to Look 13

Chapter 3: Defining What You Like   17
    Be Realistic 19
    Be Thorough 20

Part II: Select 23

Chapter 4: Who Says It, What They Say, and How to Take It   25
    Who Says It 26
    What They Say 28
    How to Take It 30

Chapter 5: Comparison Shopping for Art   35
    Why Everyone Doesn't Comparison Shop 35
    Established versus Offbeat Resources 36
    Locating Galleries That Sell What You Want 37
    Making Contact 39

Chapter 6: Dealer Dealings   43
    Characteristics of Good Art Dealers 46
    Dealers to Watch Out For 47

Chapter 7: What to Do Inside Art Galleries   53
    Gallery Interiors versus the Rest of the World 54
    Art Gallery Back Rooms, Storage Areas, and Offices 55
    Art Gallery Libraries 56
    Tips on Recognizing the Best (and Worst) Galleries for You 57

Chapter 8: How to Be a Good Customer   61
              Things Dealers Like   61
              Things Dealers Don't Like   63
Chapter 9: How *Not* to Buy Art   67

Part III: Research   75

Chapter 10: Researching an Artist   77
              How to Locate Biographical Data   79
              How to Interpret the Results of Artist Research   83
              Assessing the Facts   84
              What to Do When You Come
                Up Empty-Handed   86
Chapter 11: Researching a Work of Art   91
Chapter 12: Provenance is Profit   101
              What Provenance Means   101
              Acquiring and Maintaining Provenance   105
Chapter 13: Damaged Art   111
              Learning about Types of Damage   112
              How Much Damage Is Considered
                Acceptable?   114
              Inspecting Condition Before You Buy   116
              Maintaining Your Art   117
Chapter 14: Forgers and Forgeries   121
              Know Your Artists   122
              How Forgers Sell   122
              Learning to Detect Forgeries   123
              Spotting the Art and Craft of Forgery   124
              Some Methods for Checking Paintings   127
              Forged Limited Edition Prints   128
              Forged Sculptures   129

Part IV: Buy   133

Chapter 15: The Economics of Art: An Introduction   135
              The Liquidity of Art   136
              Unique Aspects of the Art Economy   137
              Art as an Investment   138
              Why Some Art Increases in Value   139
Chapter 16: How to Evaluate Art Prices   141
              Asking the Seller   142

Checking Art Auction Prices 143
Approximating a Work's Auction Value 146
Consulting No-Conflict-of-Interest Resources 151
Using Art Price Guides as Research Tools 153

Chapter 17: Negotiating a Purchase   157
How a Negotiating Relationship Evolves 158
Proper Bargaining Etiquette: Dos and Don'ts 159
Advanced Negotiating 161

Chapter 18: The Buy: What It Involves and How to Make It   165
Paying For Your Art 165
Documenting Your Purchases 166
Return and Exchange Arrangements 168
Art Buys That Are Less Than Ideal 171

Chapter 19: Action at the Auction   175
Auctions versus Art Galleries 176
Common Misconceptions about Auctions 178
Who Bids at Auction and Why? 180
Auction Plus Points: Why Buy Art at Aution? 181
How to Buy at Auction 183
Conclusion 186

Appendixes 187

1: Art Periodicals   189
2: Art Reference Sources   190
3: Significant American Auction Houses   196
4: American Appraiser Associations   197
5: Major American Art Dealer Associations   198
6: Art Reference Booksellers   199

Index   201

Acknowledgments

A number of art experts, art collectors, and art business professionals aided me in the writing of this book. Much of their help was in the form of discussions; debates; and the sharing of beliefs, feelings, and opinions about how art should be bought, sold, and collected. Their feedback on so many different topics was instrumental in the completion of my task. I thank the following people for contributing to this book:

First, thanks go to my wife, Louise. Without her support, this book would have been considerably more difficult to complete.

Special thanks go to all the people from across the country who respond to my "Art Talk" column with their letters and calls. You are the ones who gave me the idea for *Buy Art Smart* and who continue to guide me in my writing with your questions and requests for information about art and art collecting.

Thanks also go (in no particular order) to the art librarians at the main branches of the San Francisco and Oakland public libraries, the art librarians at the San Francisco Museum of Modern Art, Mark Simpson and Sally Mills of the Fine Arts Museums of San Francisco, Charles Campbell, Stacey Roman and Susan Friedewald of Butterfield and Butterfield, Scot Levitt, D. J. Puffert, Scott Haskins, Bill Currier, Edan Hughes, Jonathan Leichtling, Tom Hoepf of *Antique Week*, John Garzoli, Lisa Peters of Montgomery Gallery, Ruth Braunstein, Dr. Joseph Baird, F. E. Keeler, Steve Newman, Ray Lewis, Mark and Colleen Hoffman of Maxwell Galleries, Tom Rarick, George Stern, and Harris Stewart.

BUY ART SMART

Introduction

Buying art was once a fairly simple procedure. The few people who could afford it or, for that matter, were even interested in owning it, bought what they loved and bought it almost exclusively for aesthetic reasons—to enrich their lives and beautify their surroundings. Sophisticated collectors were few and far between, and ideas such as art fluctuating in value over time or being bought and sold like stocks and bonds were basically unheard of. In recent years, however, buying art has become increasingly complex, specialized, and financially oriented.

The days of casually shopping around and buying whatever happens to look good are gone—or at least they should be. Those old adages of "I buy with my eye," or "I know what I like," or "It looks good to me and that's all I care about" are no longer sufficient preparation for collecting in these days of art business sophistication and diversity.

For one thing, art is expensive. If costs were no more than several hundred dollars per item, this book wouldn't be necessary. Anyone could go out and buy whatever he or she wanted to with minimal risk. But art prices start in the low hundreds and spiral rapidly upward from there. When that kind of money is at stake, you've got to be careful how you spend it.

To further complicate matters, dollar values of art are not determined in a straightforward manner. Art is not priced by the pound or the square inch. Artists do not work by the hour; art dealers do not have set markups or standardized brokerage fees. As a result, you cannot tell whether a work of art is fairly priced simply by looking at it.

Take, for example, an average 24- by 36-inch painting hanging on the wall of an average art gallery. This painting is composed of a piece of canvas, four wooden stretcher bars, some staples or nails, a little paint, and a frame. The cost of these raw materials rarely exceeds $100, most of which is for the frame. Let's say the gallery is asking $3,000 for the painting. You would prefer that if you buy this work of art, you get something more like a $3,000 painting and less like $100 worth of raw materials that happen to resemble a painting. And this is only the beginning.

Here you are, ready to spend money, ready to buy art. Consider three situations you could easily encounter:

1. You see a painting you like at Triple-A Fine Arts Gallery. It is a handsome coastal sunset priced at $500. Three-Star International Gallery, just down

the street, has a virtually identical coastal sunset by a different artist priced at $5,000. Which painting makes a better buy?

2. You're at an antiques show. You are attracted to a watercolor of flowers in a vase signed "Rembrandt Van Gogh." Its owner, Bert Pim of Regency Plus Antiques, informs you that Rembrandt Van Gogh watercolors sell for lots of money. Bert goes on to say that he bought this picture out of a fabulous old estate where every piece in the house was a quality antique. He expects it to sell fast because, according to him, the asking price is a bargain. Do you buy it?

3. Auguste Le Soir, owner of European Palace Fine Arts, catches you eyeing a Monty Morton sculpture. Le Soir remarks that European Palace represents Monty exclusively and that the gallery has sold fifteen Morton sculptures in the past year, each for over $8,000. Le Soir then hands you a beautiful, full-color gallery brochure on Monty's life and work. You are impressed that Mortons are owned by, among others, Countess Esmerildo of Tyrolia and the International Gherkin Corporation. Should you buy one?

Questions like these do not have instant answers, but they do have answers—definite answers. And, by the time you finish this book, you'll know what they are.

True, art concerns aesthetics, beauty, mystery, passion, drama, magic, and other intangibles. True, you buy a work of art because still more personal intangibles come into play, such as what the piece means to you, how it affects you on different levels, and how it makes you feel when you look at it. *However,* while buying art is unquestionably a personal emotional experience, no rule states that when you enter a gallery you check your intellect at the door.

Shopping for art is like shopping for any other product. Experienced art collectors will tell you this. When you buy art smart, the beauty and mystery of fine art and the creative process which brings it into existence are tempered by the hard realities of free enterprise and competition in the marketplace.

Part I: Identify

CHAPTER 1

What This Book Is About

There is no right or wrong art; there is no right or wrong reason for wanting to own art; and there is no right or wrong way to go about buying art. With these thoughts in mind, you are about to begin a book that deals not in rights and wrongs, but rather in suggestions and recommendations which stem from two basic assumptions about people who buy art:

- People prefer to buy good quality art.

- People prefer to pay fair prices for the art they buy.

All techniques and methods described in this text follow directly from these assumptions as a starting point. If you are like the great majority of art buyers, you too want good quality at fair prices—you want to buy art smart.

Unfortunately, most beginners feel anywhere from inadequate to totally helpless about the subject of buying art "intelligently." Worse yet, they have little faith in their abilities to ever accomplish this goal. To them, art is a mysterious and incomprehensible commodity, the secrets of which are understood only by art dealers, art scholars, and other specialized experts.

As a result, beginners all buy art in pretty much the same way—impulsively. They buy what they like, or think they like, wherever they happen to see it for sale and the first time they lay eyes on it. Any questions they might have are put to the sellers; whatever answers they get are instantly accepted. No further efforts are involved. They buy this way because they aren't aware that alternative methods exist and that they can actually control their art-collecting destinies.

Here's the truth: *You—or anyone else—can research and evaluate any work of art you see for sale entirely on your own and determine whether you are spending your money wisely if you choose to buy it.* Everything you need to know is laid out right here in an easy-to-understand, easy-to-follow, and logical progression.

FACTS ABOUT THIS BOOK

This Book Is A Beginning. However involved you decide to get with art, what you are about to learn will serve as an introduction. You can spend a lifetime mastering the skills necessary to build a substantive art collection, but first you need a good solid foundation—and this book happens to be a great place to get it.

This Book Is A Consumer Guide to Buying Art. It approaches art from a product standpoint, and it approaches the buying and selling of art from a business standpoint. As in any other consumer situation, when you buy art you deserve to be treated fairly, you deserve to know what you're buying, and you deserve a quality product for your money.

This Is A Generic Art Book. It is specially designed to guide you through the intricacies of the art world regardless of your tastes. No matter what you want in art, the procedures for familiarizing yourself with its peculiarities, learning about the artists who create it, and learning how to buy it effectively are remarkably similar in many ways.

The Term "Art" As Used In This Book Is Whatever You Want It to Be. Whether your interests center on Old Master paintings, sporting scene lithographs, abstract sculptures, wildlife prints, etchings of Paris street scenes, or _____ (you fill in the blank with what you want to collect), this book will serve you equally well. The only requirement for our purposes here is that the art be original and artist-created, not mass-produced by mechanical means in a factory-type setting.

This Book Favors No Artists, and It Favors No Art. In order to keep you from becoming biased or unduly influenced in the direction of your collecting, the artist names you see in the text are fabricated, and facts about artist careers are fabricated. Only occasionally, in examples at the ends of chapters, are actual artists' names mentioned, and only then to make points about how the art business works, not about those artists. Words describing different types of art (paintings, lithographs, sculptures, etchings, watercolors, etc.) are also used interchangeably throughout the book. All are treated equally, the point being that the entire text is applicable to all art and that no medium is better to collect than any other.

This Book Applies to Art In All Price Ranges. Whether you are chasing after multimillion dollar masterworks or have a per-piece budget of $200, the ways you learn about and ultimately buy your art are essentially the same.

This Book Introduces You to the Way the Art World Works. It teaches you general truths about art, the art community, and the business of buying, selling, and collecting. Wherever you go to buy art, whoever you meet in the process, and whatever you hear, the great majority of what you read here will apply to your experiences.

This Book Is About Safe, Sensible, Low-Risk Ways to Begin Collecting. A conservative approach is necessary, because without experience, you can be taken advantage of in too many ways. You can overpay, get stuck with forgeries, buy inferior pieces, be fooled by get-rich-quick schemes, buy art with severe condition problems, and so on. Once you build yourself a good solid base of knowledge from which to operate—once you master the fundamentals—you can branch out, take risks, and experiment with more advanced methods of collecting.

This Book Is Primarily About Buying Art at Established Art Galleries. These are the best places for novices to begin collecting because galleries provide personal attention, offer ample learning opportunities, and protect buyers with guarantees that are difficult to get elsewhere. You will find occasional references throughout the book to alternative sources for buying, such as flea markets, garage and estate sales, art liquidations, resale outlets, auctions, and so on. The message about those resources, here and elsewhere, is that you're welcome to explore them, but you really should wait until you know what you're doing before you patronize them. You can use what you learn here to buy art anywhere, but when you're just starting out, galleries are the safest way to go.

This Book Is About *Collecting* Art, Not "Investing" In It. It is not about making money. If anything, it's about keeping you from losing money. Those of you who don't have a fundamental love, appreciation, fascination, and passion for art to begin with—feelings that are totally unrelated to dollars and cents—should probably get out now, because in the long run you'll lose. Although financial aspects of art are important and will be dicussed at length, they should never be the primary consideration in deciding whether or not to buy a work of art.

THE FOUR STEPS TO BUYING ART SMART

A lot can happen in the time interval between the moment you get the inclination to buy art and the moment you exit an art gallery with your first purchase in tow. You can buy at random and hope for the best, or you can order your activities, logically proceed from one step to the next, and assure yourself the best possible outcome. This second approach is also known as buying art smart. If you happen to be of the buy-art-smart persuasion, the way to accomplish this goal involves your following four important steps exemplified by four key words, as described below.

Identify. The first step to follow once you get the urge to buy art is to *identify* those types of art that attract you the most. You need concrete ideas of what your tastes are, of what in art really affects you in a deep and meaningful way. Part I of this book teaches you how to identify the art that's right for you.

Select. Your next step is to locate and *select* specific works of art for possible purchase, art that appeals to you according to the guidelines laid out in Part I. In order to accomplish this, you need a working knowledge of how the art business operates. Familiarizing yourself with the art community, art personalities, art dealers, art galleries, and learning your responsibilities as an art buyer are all parts of the selection process. Part II of this book teaches you how to understand and navigate the art business in a way that maximizes your chances for selecting those works of art that are best for you.

Research. Once you make your selections, you have to learn about them by *researching* them. In order to make informed decisions about whether or not you really want to own the works of art you are considering, you need to acquire specific information about the art itself, the artists who created it, and any other general background information relevant to that art. Part III of this book teaches you art research techniques.

Buy. All works of art that remain appealing to you at this final stage in your decision-making process become subject to one last consideration: price. Before you make that ultimate determination to *buy* or not to buy, you need to understand the dollars and cents consequences of your actions. You also need instruction in how to complete whatever purchases you do end up making—that is, how to complete them to your best advantage. Part IV, the final part of this book, teaches you how to evaluate art prices and how to buy art advantageously.

Identify, select, research, and buy—that's what buying art smart is all about. *Buy Art Smart* will not transform you into an instant art expert—that takes time, effort, and plenty of practice. It will, however, transform you into an informed consumer, protect you from making bad buys, and help you locate the best art for your money. So take some time to read this book, follow the instructions, and learn art business basics. Don't rush out to spend your money until you have a handle on how to spend it wisely.

Seasoned collectors will tell you that the "work" involved in identifying, selecting, and researching the right art for their collections is not really work at all, but more like adventure. In fact, almost all of these collectors will go on to say that the final act of buying is anticlimatic in relation to the events that lead up to those moments. Collectors across the board further agree that the learning process is self-perpetuating—the more they learn and the better they get at collecting, the greater their rewards and the more they want to learn in the future.

But we're getting a little ahead of ourselves here. At this stage all you know is that you want to buy art. Let's get started and learn how to identify those types of art that you would most enjoy collecting.

CHAPTER 2
Discovering What You Like

The great majority of people who decide to buy art are relatively unaware of the incredible variety that's available for purchase. Their tastes are the products of happenstance in the form of limited, arbitrary encounters with art. They operate according to preconceived notions about art collecting, art buying, and what the art they want to own looks like—notions that they've held for years, or even decades.

Take a few moments here to jot down *your* preconceived notions. Include what you think the art you're interested in buying looks like, who the artists are, where you might go to buy it, how much it costs, and any other relevant information. Be as specific and detailed as possible, and *save these notes*. They define your official starting point and will serve as a reminder of where you were when you began this book.

Done writing? Good. Now take your piece of paper, fold it up, put it in a drawer, and forget about it. While you're at it, imagine putting everything else you know about art into that drawer and forgetting about it also. Your current knowledge may well come in handy later, but for the time being, let's start with a blank slate. Approach your quest to identify what you like as though you've never read or heard a thing about art before in your life, as though you have no opinions about it whatsoever.

Whatever you think, forget it for now. Don't let your brain get in the way. With brain in full gear, you look at a painting, print, or sculpture and hear little voices in your head saying things like "My friends will stop speaking to me if I buy this," or "This thing will never increase in value," or "I have no idea who this artist is—her art can't be any good." Screening out all this interference allows you to begin at the very beginning and survey your most basic gut reactions to art.

An empty mind permits you see, feel, and experience pure emotion. The art controls you. You do not filter your response to the art through a belief system that may or may not have a reasonable basis. By letting your raw feelings guide you, you take the first big step in identifying what you really like. After all is said and done, of course, you may find that you are attracted to the exact same art you were before you started, but then again, you may discover that your true tastes are for art that you never imagined you could ever appreciate.

LOOK, LOOK, LOOK

Now that your mind is out of the picture, let's get art into the picture. You've got to familiarize yourself with the product you intend to purchase. *Your first assignment in the identification process: Get out there and see as much art and as many different kinds of art as you can.*

Either you can take a systematic approach to your looking and see one particular type of art at a time, or you can see many different types in a day. Whatever you feel comfortable doing is fine, but remember, don't be selective in your viewing—look at everything everywhere.

Visit places specifically to see art, such as museums, historical societies, art galleries, local art associations, and corporate collections. But don't stop there. Wherever your day-to-day activities take you—shopping malls, banks, doctors' offices, hotel lobbies, restaurants—keep a constant eye to the walls, the pedestals, and the display areas. At this early stage, the art you see in a shopping mall is just as important to study as what you see at a museum.

See old art, new art, abstract art, big art, little art, bright art, dark art. Look at paintings, sculptures, etchings, prints, and watercolors. Look at "works of art" that you're not even sure are art. Once again—*look at everything.* Don't try to understand it, analyze it, read about it, find out who the artists are, figure out what it is or how it's made, or ask other people what they think about it. Just plop yourself down in front of it and look. Monitor your reactions to it—that's all.

Do you like it or not? Does it make you feel happy, sad, calm, angry, exhilarated? Do you love it or hate it or have no reaction to it at all? Does it make you think about certain issues? Does it transport you to other realities, faraway places? These are the internal reactions that you are looking to define.

Two additional pointers:

- *Study art you hate, as well as art you like.* Recognizing what you want to avoid is just as important as recognizing what you love.

- *Don't ignore certain types of art you are already familiar with because you think know what your reactions will be and believe that nothing about those reactions will ever change.* That's your brain getting in the way again. View it as though you are seeing it for the very first time.

HOW TO LOOK

Looking at art means more than giving casual glances as you pass it by. You've got to spend time studying individual pieces.

Stand up close and focus on small areas of the art. Stand back and look at the whole thing. Stick your nose right up to the canvas or wood or paper or bronze and study the most minute details. Back away slowly and watch how the art changes. Move so far away that the art fades into its surroundings.

Look at the colors, subject matters, sizes, styles, frames, pedestals. Look at single brushstrokes on a painting, single lines on an etching, single details on a sculpture. Look at the materials making up the art; see how it's put together.

If you happen to see something you really like, note what it is, where you saw it, how it looks, and why it attracts you—nothing more. You'll have plenty of opportunity to return and learn more about it later.

Resist the temptation to speak with people about whatever you're looking at. Start asking questions and you'll be right back in that rut of letting your mind or the minds of others control your responses. Avoid exposing yourself to opinions on what's good, what's bad, what to collect, or what to avoid. At this formative stage, no one has the inside line on what's best for you more than you do.

Don't read literature or brochures about the art you are looking at. Don't look at nameplates, titles, or price tags. Pay no attention to the names of artists or how famous they are. All this information interferes with your gut feelings. Suppose, for example, you see a painting and hate the way it looks. Then you find out that Picasso painted it and it's selling for $14 million. Do you change your mind all of a sudden and decide that you really like it? Of course not!

Remember, all you're doing here is looking and feeling. You are not committing yourself in any way; you can change your mind about what you like at any time. You are simply getting in touch with how you feel when you look at various types of art. *The goal of "looking without thinking" is this: By experiencing a little bit of everything that's out there and taking some time to study it in detail, you begin to acquire strength of conviction and begin to identify what really thrills you.*

Out of all the millions of art pieces that have ever been and have yet to be created, you will choose to own maybe one, maybe five, maybe one hundred. And you'll choose them because they mean something special to you and you alone. Now is the time to acquire a feel for where that special meaning lies by identifying what qualities in art attract you the most.

Example 1: The most sophisticated collectors I know are the ones who spend the most time looking at art. Some focus only on the art they collect, while others are more adventurous and are constantly on the lookout for something new and fascinating. One man in particular makes a point of looking at and studying a much greater amount and wider range of art than he collects. He stays in shape, so to speak, and, as a result, is able to evaluate many different types of art on a variety of levels, whether he collects them or not.

This man began by collecting impressionist paintings by American artists, moved on to regionalist art of the 1930s and 1940s, and has recently become fascinated by abstract and abstract expressionist works. By keeping informed about current events and studying whatever art is brought to his attention—whether he knows anything about it or not—he has developed an uncanny ability for spotting new trends in the marketplace ahead of most other collectors. One big payoff here is that he is consistently able to buy ahead of the market while selection is still good and prices are still reasonable.

Example 2: An incredible amount of art is bought by people who have never bothered to formally identify their true preferences. They buy because someone tells them to, because they think they're going to make a bundle of money when they resell, because they think the artists are "famous," and so on. Buying art this way hurts just about everyone:

- The buyers themselves suffer because they are being controlled by outside forces. They have no idea whether or not they are buying what they like.

- Artists suffer. Rather than selecting from the great variety of art that artists produce, inexperienced buyers put their money into those few names they already recognize, names that happen to be the most trendy, are hyped the most, get the best news coverage, and so on. Many fine artists who are not extremely publicity-oriented have difficulty selling their art because people follow the glitz and glamour and buy like sheep.

- Dealers who deal in quality art suffer. The market gets flooded with art that is not necessarily good but that satisfies mass tastes—whatever buyers think is the thing to buy at the moment. At worst, money goes to slick businesspeople who know more about marketing what's hot than they do about art.

What's important here is that you learn about what's available, pinpoint your tastes, cultivate an independence of intention, and avoid jumping into the market before you have a good solid footing. Develop confidence in yourself. Then begin buying.

A LOOK AHEAD

Once you start to get an idea of what the qualities of art that attract you are, you'll be ready to get practical—that is, to let your brain back into the picture. Putting thoughts to your feelings suddenly becomes necessary because that is the only way you'll be able to communicate your needs, acquire information, and, in the end, buy art. Your next step in the identification process, therefore, is defining what it is you really want to collect. This aspect of collecting is discussed in the chapter that follows.

CHAPTER 3

Defining What You Like

So far, you have experienced art on a purely emotional level, evaluating how it looks and feels to you with no interference from the brain, that is, the intellect. You have seen and noted particular works of art that possess a certain magic for you, that impress you in a way you find appealing. Defining what you like means putting the characteristics and qualities of this special art into words.

Not only do you have to define it, but you have to be specific. The better you are able to pinpoint your preferences, the better the art community is able to understand and serve you.

Begin this procedure by reviewing any notes you took during your Chapter 1 adventures. Return to locations where you saw art you liked. View that art again, and find out basic information about it. If you have questions about specific works of art, have experts such as curators, art dealers, or experienced collectors explain and clarify whatever details you're unsure of. Record all relevant data for future reference. Avoid getting involved in any serious discussions about art (it's a little premature for that), and confine your fact-gathering mission the following:

- Find out where the art originates. Is it American, European, South American, Japanese? Is it from Detroit, from Texas, from New York?

- Find out the names of the artists.

- Note when the art dates from. Is it from the nineteenth century, the early twentieth century, current times, or some other period?

- Note what style or styles the individual works of art are. Are they abstract? Realistic? Impressionistic? Surreal?

- Identify the media the works are executed in. Are the works watercolors, bronzes, oil paintings, etchings, color lithographs, wood carvings, and so on?

- Identify the subject matters. Are they landscapes? Seascapes? Still lifes? City scenes? Busts of famous politicians? Geometric abstracts?

- Find out the dollar values of art that is for sale or in the private sector (as opposed to that on permanent display in museums).

- Note any other relevant physical characteristics of your chosen works, such as what sizes, shapes, and colors they are.

Once you have assembled this information, combine it into a concise opening statement that you can make to anyone who is interested in knowing what you prefer in your art. As conversations progress, you can fill in the additional details as required. Here are some examples of good opening statements:

"I'm interested in contemporary oil paintings of spring scenes in the French countryside."

"I love New Orleans scenes by Louisiana artists, painted before 1920."

"I'm looking for abstract sculptures executed by New York City artists between 1930 and 1950."

"I want to buy etchings and lithographs of sporting scenes that have waterfowl in them, preferably ducks."

Make sure your statement provides adequate introductory information about your needs. Suppose, for example, you are in an art gallery and the owner asks what you are interested in collecting. You answer: "Seascapes." You feel perfectly comfortable with that answer because the central feature of every work of art you like is that it has a large body of water in it. But if you think for a moment, "seascapes" happens to cover a huge amount of territory. Your statement is too general; the dealer has virtually no information to work with. He or she could show you hundreds of seascapes, none of which you might find acceptable.

The dealer has no idea whether you want coastal scenes, clipper ships tossing about on stormy seas, or peaceful sunsets over tropical beaches; large pictures or small ones; bright pictures or dark ones; contemporary examples or ones that were painted decades ago. You can only carry on a constructive conversation about your tastes in art when you have a good opener and plenty of specifics to follow it up with.

Don't worry that defining your likes too narrowly at this early stage will eliminate huge amounts of art from consideration before you even get started. This is not the case, and, in fact, the opposite often happens. Once you begin focusing in on specifics, you realize that a lot more is available within that particular realm of collecting than you ever imagined existed. And remember, just because you define your interests now doesn't mean that you must stick to them for the rest of your life. You can modify your opening statement or change your preferences at any time.

The general rules for buying art are pretty much the same no matter what you decide to collect. By setting an initial direction now and following through to the point of purchase, you acquire the basic skills necessary to form a quality collection of any type of art you may eventually choose to focus on.

BE REALISTIC

An important part of defining your likes is making them workable in the real world of art collecting. By setting realistic, reachable goals for yourself, you maximize the chances of your being able to find exactly the art you are looking for. If your preferences in art are great in theory but impractical in terms of collecting, you've got to adjust them appropriately. Below are some factors you should take into consideration.

Make Sure That You Can Afford What You Want to Collect. As soon as possible, determine your budget; decide approximately how much money you are willing to spend per work of art. If the art that thrills you the most is too expensive, look for something more affordable that has similar characteristics to those favorites.

Suppose, for example, that you love French Impressionist paintings, but your per-piece budget is only $5,000. Average French Impressionist works start in the hundreds of thousands of dollars each and quickly get up into the millions. For your $5,000, you can't even buy a scribble on a scrap of paper. You could solve this problem by looking instead for pictures that approximate the look of those you like and sell in the $5,000 range. Your opening statement could be: "I want to collect paintings done in the manner of the French Impressionists that cost between $3,000 and $5,000 each."

Make Sure That You Can Buy A Reasonably Good Piece of Art on Your Per-Piece Budget. If you can't afford good-quality examples of what you like the most, lower your sights accordingly. Collectors across the board will tell you that regardless of your budget, you should buy as close to the top of your chosen area of collecting as you can.

For example, if good-quality pieces of the art you like the most cost $8,000 to $10,000 each and you only have $2,000 to spend, you won't be able to get very much for your money. You'll be forced to buy closer to the bottom of the market for this art than the top. Find a kind of art you like just as much for which $2,000 buys the best or at least a better example of what's available, not a mediocre one.

Make Sure That What You Like Is Readily Available and That You Have A Good Selection to Choose From. You won't be able to build a quality collection if the type of art you're looking for is so rare that it hardly ever comes onto the market.

Make Sure That You Like What You Do for Art Reasons, Not Money Reasons. Buy because you love the way the art looks, you are fascinated by the history behind it, and so on. If you like the art you do because you think it will go up in value, think again. For one thing, only a small percentage of art increases in value over time. For another, getting all caught up in money matters can destroy the fun of collecting.

Keep Your Preferences Conservative at First. Focus on art that dealers and collectors generally accept as being collectible. The more you learn and the more experienced you become, the more experimental you can afford to be in your collecting.

BE THOROUGH

Be complete and thorough when defining your likes; don't overlook any important details. You must be fully aware of the qualities you want in your art and of the basic principles that will be guiding your buying. The truth is that some art buyers are not aware of these things, and, consequently, the art they end up owning is quite different from the art that they originally set out to collect.

Suppose, for example, that you meet a collector who tells you, "I love to collect paintings of Florida coastal scenes done between 1890 and 1980." You visit him at his home, he gives you a tour of his collection, and at first glance, all his pictures seem to be exactly what he told you they were. But as he presents each piece and describes it, he finishes with statements like, "Paintings by this artist sell for $750 and up—I paid only $150 for mine at the flea market," or "I got this one at an estate sale for a tenth of what it's worth."

Whether or not this collector originally intended it, a guiding principle behind his collecting—and one that belongs in his opening statement—is that he selects only those coastal scenes done between 1890 and 1980 that he can buy cheaply enough to brag to his friends and acquaintances about what great bargains he got. A more appropriate statement about his collecting would be, "I love to buy Florida coastal scenes done between 1890 and 1980 that I can get for much less than they're really worth," or "I collect bargain paintings that happen to be Florida coastal scenes done between 1890 and 1980." He cannot legitimately title his collection "Florida Coastal Scenes Painted between 1890 and 1980."

This fellow may need to reevaluate his buying strategies if he's not fully aware of how much the bargain requirement is controlling his selection process. By limiting his purchases to "bargain" paintings, he automatically eliminates all nonbargains from consideration. This could result in his compromising quality for price and depriving himself of important coastal scenes or art by particular artists that simply can't be found at bargain prices. His obsession with bargains adversely affects his collecting.

Here are examples of two other constraints that can and do significantly alter the intended courses of many a collection:

1. Only selecting works of art that a particular person—wife, mother-in-law, best friend, employer, etc.—approves of. The resulting collection would be more indicative of the tastes of the approving person than of the collector.

2. Buying all art from a single gallery. A collector who patronizes only one gallery does not really buy what he or she likes; that collector buys what the gallery likes.

A LOOK AHEAD

Identifying what you like, tempering it with the realities of your collecting situation, and defining it in a manner that the art community understands completes the first step in the process of buying art. The next step—which is the goal of Part II—involves your selecting specific works of art for possible purchase according to your requirements. In order to make the best choices, however, you need basic training; that is, you need an introduction to how the art world operates.

Part II: Select

Selecting a work of art for possible purchase is simple. Since you are now able to identify what you like, all you have to do is walk into a gallery, take a look around, see something interesting, and say to yourself, "I wouldn't mind owning that." Selection process completed.

The hard part is locating that gallery in the first place; knowing what to do once you get there; being able to tell whether you have encountered a good dealer or a bad one; effectively interacting with anyone you meet before, during, and after your visit; and knowing how to behave in order to maximize the quality of that visit. Consequently, the goal of Part II is not to teach you how to select art—you can do that already—but rather to provide you with the information you need in order to assure that your selection process has a positive outcome. Part II is a basic course in understanding and navigating through the art community. The truth is that you probably won't come face to face with and select the art that's right for you until you know how to get around.

CHAPTER 4

Who Says It, What They Say, and How to Take It

So far, you've kept pretty quiet about your art interests and intent to buy. Everything you've done, you've done pretty much on your own. Keeping your contacts brief has allowed you to wander from place to place, make initial observations about what you like, and acquire basic information about it with little or no interference from outsiders. Sooner or later, though, you must deepen your contacts, make your intentions known in greater detail, and progress toward buying art.

Once you begin to do this, the way the art world relates to you changes. You are no longer a looker—you are now a participant. People start taking vested interests in how you should think, feel, and react to art. They declare, expound, criticize, hold court, pass judgments, share beliefs, emote, foretell the future, and say whatever comes to mind regarding your particular situation. They want a say in your selection process.

Speaking with others about art can be quite difficult at first. You hear many different things from many different people, and you're never quite sure how to respond. You don't really know who's right and who's wrong, who knows what they're talking about and who doesn't. You have little choice but to take whatever you hear at face value because you don't yet have the knowledge to analyze and digest.

So what do you do? You jump right in and start talking. You tell people exactly what you know and exactly what you're looking for. That's the best practice you can get and the only sensible way to begin. By participating in conversation after conversation, you eventually figure out how to evaluate what you are hearing, extract the information you need, formulate your own opinions, and select the art that's right for you.

When you don't know much about art, however, and the people you are talking with do, you are at a constant disadvantage. They find out more about you faster than you do about them. They control the conversations and have a variety of options in responding to whatever you say, while you have very few.

Imagine putting on a pair of boxing gloves and stepping into the ring with a professional fighter. He can give you a painless and highly educational lesson in how to box, he can exit the ring without saying a word and leave you standing there, he can pound you to a pulp, and so on. You can run, plead for mercy, or put up your gloves and see how long you last—and that's about it. Depending on the fighter's response to your situation, you can leave the ring knowing more than when you stepped into it, you can leave learning nothing, or you can end up staring at the ceiling.

This is similar to what you encounter as you begin to speak with people about art. You step into the art ring with professional after professional, tell them about your situation, and listen to their responses. Some help you, others tell you nothing, and a few take the opportunity to hinder you or manipulate you to their own ends.

Your task is to separate the helpers from the hinderers as quickly as possible and to use what you hear to locate the art you want and advance your collecting. Sooner or later, you acquire the necessary skills to assess accurately all that people tell you. This chapter is about how to make it sooner.

WHO SAYS IT

Figuring out whose views to accept and how much to accept them is difficult at first. Everyone can sound like they know what they're talking about as long as they present themselves in a reasonably competent and trustworthy manner. You can't really apply any quick and easy rules to diagnosing a situation, but you don't have to operate blind, either. Knowing a little about the structure of art interactions comes in handy here.

To begin with, be aware of conflicts of interest. In any conversation, know when other people stand to benefit from having you see things their way and having you select the art they want you to select. The greater the profit potential is for a person—monetarily, psychologically, or otherwise— the more inclined that person is to give you a biased view of art.

Art scholars, museum curators, and others who are not involved with the art *business,* but rather with the academic, scholarly, and historical aspects of art, can usually be relied upon for accurate, unbiased information. They do not profit from having you believe their views about art, do not ordinarily take sides, and purposely steer clear of the business aspects of art. When you ask their advice, they attempt to present the issues fairly and allow you to make the necessary decisions for yourself.

Individuals involved with the art business are different. People who sell art for a living, such as art dealers, gallery employees, and auction house staff people, profit directly by having you believe what they believe. With such people, you have to be a little more careful about who and what you listen to and believe. Most sellers represent their art fairly and tell you exactly what you need to know, but remember that the possibility of their making sales always looms on the horizon. If they can influence your selection process, they will.

Much of what sellers tell you relates specifically to the art they sell. Even when you speak with them casually, outside of direct selling situations, be aware that they believe very strongly in what they sell and present consistently positive cases for owning their type of art and less positive cases for owning other types of art. They want you to like what they like, whether you buy it or not.

Keep in mind also that sellers don't always know that much about types of art outside their fields. They know plenty about what they sell, but they are not necessarily well-informed about what other people sell. When you ask sellers about art they don't deal in, you won't always get accurate answers. But you will get answers, answers that you should always corroborate with more knowledgeable experts before accepting.

Sellers are most helpful in educating you about the art and artists they represent. When you speak with them, keep conversations focused on their specialties. Whether or not their type of art turns out to be the right art for you, they can tell you just about everything you need to know about it.

Art collectors are much like sellers in that they also prefer having you see art the way they do. Suppose, for instance, that a private collector is giving you a tour of his collection. He believes certain things about the art he has collected, and it's in his best interests that you believe them, too.

Let's say you agree with his views on collecting (that is, you approve of what's in his collection) and decide to select and buy similar art for yourself. By doing so, you indirectly increase the value of his art by increasing the demand for that art in the marketplace. The more people that agree with this collector's views on collecting and buy what he buys, the greater the demand for that type of art becomes.

This collector also benefits from your support in a psychological sense—you make him feel good about himself and his collection when you agree with him. If you don't see eye to eye on a particular point, he'll most likely attempt to convince you he's right. Knowing that you disagree with him about the art he has chosen to buy may make him feel uncomfortable because he may feel that perhaps he has not spent his money wisely.

Collectors feel strongly about what they collect, and that's fine, but once again, you've got to decide whether believing them works as well for you as it does for them. They may have quality collections and know what they're talking about—in which case, you're safe following their leads. On the other hand, they may think they have bought wisely when, in fact, they haven't. They may think their art is worth a lot more than it actually is, and they may think it's a lot better than it actually is. You certainly don't want to follow any leads in either of those circumstances.

Be careful when speaking with collectors, for the simple reason that they frequently do not know as much about art as full-time art experts. They collect in their spare time and do not spend their lives amassing knowledge about art the way that people in the business or museum curators and art scholars do. Furthermore, their focus is much narrower than that of most experts. Although some may speak with strong conviction and sound like they know everything there is to know, be cautious and check out what they tell you before accepting it as fact.

Speak with as many dealers, collectors, auction house and art gallery employees, museum curators, and other experts as possible. By listening to everyone, you acquire a well-balanced picture of what you want to select and eventually buy. Accumulating information from a great variety of sources protects you from coming under the influence of any one or two in particular. Weigh all points of view on a continuing basis so you can progressively strengthen your convictions.

WHAT THEY SAY

You hear plenty about art as you move through the art world from one person to the next. What you hear can be broken down into three basic categories:

- Facts about art and artists

- Emotional reactions to artists or works of art

- Market information about artists or works of art

Facts Are Easy to Evaluate. They are either true or false and can almost always be verified simply and directly. Sometimes the people who state the facts offer that verification themselves. Other times, you have to corroborate what you hear by independently contacting art experts or researching at museums, libraries, and other resources.

The operative word here is *verify*. Any time you are presented with new or unfamiliar information, check it out—do not automatically accept it as truth. Make sure that whatever you are told is true and generally accepted by the art community. Unfortunately, you can't believe everything you hear.

For example, suppose an art dealer tells you that an artist she represents is famous. You speak with five independent art experts and several art dealers and contact several art museums to see whether you can corroborate this information. You come up with the following results: No expert has ever heard of the artist, one art dealer thinks he recognizes the name but isn't sure, and no museum can provide any information about the artist. You have to conclude that, at best, the artist is not quite as famous as the first dealer would have you believe.

Emotional Reactions to Art Are a Little More Difficult to Evaluate Than Facts. You will hear everything from raw, spontaneous reactions to the most highly informed and educated reactions (commonly referred to as art criticism). Just as you verify facts, you have to learn to verify—or, more accurately, qualify—emotional reactions in order to determine how they will influence your selection-making process. This qualifying may seem difficult, but it's not really. It just involves a little reading between the lines.

Basically, you have to figure out how qualified the people doing the reacting are. Are they knowledgeable experts who are having legitimate educated reactions, or are they casual observers who just happen to be passing by and have no idea what they are looking at? How much do the reactors know about the art they are reacting to? That's the key.

Suppose, for instance, that you are attending an art opening at Triple-A Fine Arts Gallery and overhear a man remark that the abstract paintings on display are terrible and don't even deserve to be hung in a monkey cage. You tap him on the shoulder, introduce yourself, and ask him to explain why he feels this way. He tells you that he hates bright colors and that his six-year-old daughter brings home better pictures from first-grade art class.

This is probably not an explanation you should take too seriously. It shouldn't affect your decision whether to consider one of the abstracts for purchase. If, however, this fellow goes on to say that in all his years of curating shows at the Municipal Art Museum he has never seen such amateurish work, you could have an entirely different situation on your hands. Suddenly you realize that you're dealing with someone who could well know what he's talking about. Not necessarily, though.

As a curator, he certainly qualifies as having experience in the art world, but before you can take him too seriously, you have to find out exactly where his expertise lies. If he turns out to be a curator of Greek and Roman antiquities, for instance, he may not be qualified to criticize the abstracts hanging at this opening. An expert in one field of art is not automatically qualified to judge art unrelated to that field.

If, however, he's an expert on contemporary abstracts and curates contemporary art exhibits, you listen. But don't blindly accept what he has to say. Politely insist that he support his initial reactions with facts. This is how you learn. Perhaps he'll mention a book you should read or name several other artists who accomplish the same results much more skillfully, or tell you where you can go to see really good abstracts.

When evaluating emotional reactions, always find out the answers to these three questions:

1. How qualified is the person doing the talking?

2. Can the reactions be supported with concrete proof that they are valid?

3. What is that proof?

Market Information Is the Toughest of All to Evaluate. A primary reason for this is that many people who give you price data have vested interests in what they tell you. Another problem is that you can easily be misled by people who think they know about prices but actually don't. And if that's not enough, many people are reluctant to give you price information in the first place. They want to keep what they know to themselves and use it to their advantage. Part IV of this book treats money matters in depth, but a brief summary is appropriate here.

As in evaluating emotional or critical reactions to art, you must qualify the sources of any market-related information you get. Ask people who talk prices to back up everything they say with facts. Figure out whether they have any vested interests in telling you what art is good to buy and what art isn't. Find out what experience they've had dealing with the monetary aspects of art. For example, a private collector who buys but never sells may not give you as reliable information about the art market as will someone who sells or appraises art for a living. You will also see in Part IV that standard art price references are available to the public and that you can use them to substantiate what people tell you.

HOW TO TAKE IT

At present, digesting what you hear about art is not easy. You probably don't know that much, you haven't met that many people, you're not sure whom to trust, and you haven't established any long-term relationships. You're still operating pretty much in the dark, and you never quite know how to take what people tell you.

And you hear what you hear in so many different formats. Some people seem completely trustworthy, congenial, and sincere (making you inclined to accept anything they tell you, true or not). Others have strong feelings and no qualms about imposing them on you, whether you're interested in hearing them or not. The more adamant among them can literally try to steamroll you into submission (making you inclined *not* to accept anything they tell you, true or not). Most people happen to be helpful and supportive, but not everyone is going to treat you with respect. Be prepared for anything.

Never Take What People Tell You Personally. No one is out to get you. Getting all caught up in why someone treats you disrespectfully is a monumental waste of time. Sure, you'll meet a few people who have to make your life difficult in order to feel good about themselves or prove how much they know. Consider that their problem, not yours.

Listen To and Consider *Everything* People Tell You. Get a well-rounded art education. Most people happily soak up any information that already supports their beliefs but pay little, if any, attention to divergent points of view. This is fine if you ascribe to the "ignorance is bliss" philosophy, but ignorance does not come in handy if you expect to buy art smart. Resisting or discounting opposing viewpoints before checking them out is not a healthy practice.

You don't have to believe everything you hear, follow every bit of advice that anyone gives you, or change direction at the slightest provocation. You do have to catalogue data, though. No matter whether it seems right or wrong, makes sense or not, sounds sincere or condescending, assume at first that it has value and deserves your attention.

Let's say you are interested in the artist John Doeman and are in the process of learning as much as you can about him. In your art travels, you speak with people who have heard of Doeman, people who claim to be experts on Doeman, people who have never heard of Doeman, and people who think they have heard of Doeman and will gladly comment on the artist if you would just refresh their memories as to who he is. Everyone has something to say.

So what do you do when the subject of Doeman comes up? You listen. That's the best way to go. Even if you know more about the artist than the person you are speaking with, listen. Even if someone insults you, listen. The more you listen, the more complete your picture of Doeman and his art becomes. You get an idea of where he stands as an artist, where his strengths and weaknesses lie, and what the prognosis on his future is. You learn why people like him, why they hate him, and why they don't care one way or the other.

Whenever someone gives you information about any art or artist, you learn just as much about the person giving the information (or opinion) as you do about the art. You learn whom to trust and whom to avoid, who knows what they're talking about and who doesn't. If you want to buy art smart, knowing how to evaluate people is just as important as knowing how to evaluate art.

Example 1: Some sellers say anything to sell art, and sometimes what they say is not necessarily true. One way they occasionally distort the facts is by comparing the art they have for sale to art by more famous artists. Imagine hearing any of the following reasonings from an art dealer:

> *"The painting you are thinking about buying is just as good as a Jonathan Johnson painting. Johnson's paintings sell for between $25,000 and $30,000 each. At only $3,000, that makes this painting an absolute bargain."*
>
> *"If Jonathan Johnson had painted this, it would be worth $30,000. I'm only asking $3,000 for it."*
>
> *"You can't touch a Jonathan Johnson at this price."*

None of these statements is valid. Jonathan Johnson did *not* paint the painting you like, and his price structure has nothing to do with the value of that painting. Though the two are totally unrelated, the dealer is attempting to establish a connection in order to increase the painting's attractiveness and make the asking price seem more like a bargain.

Even if the painting happens to be as good as a Jonathan Johnson, the dealer's arguments still hold no water. Much more goes into determining value than how one piece of art compares in quality to another from a visual standpoint alone. The dealer is making a frivolous and irrelevant value comparison for the sole purpose of selling you the piece art.

Carry this logic to extremes and imagine a seller telling you the following: "If Vincent Van Gogh had painted this, it would be worth $25 million. I'm only asking $3,000 for it." Does Van Gogh have anything to do with this seller's painting? Are you getting an incredible bargain if you buy it? Of course not!

Example 2: Over time, you learn who you can and cannot trust in the art business. One dealer I know does not always tell the truth. She sometimes tells me as many as five or six conflicting stories about the same work of art; other times she gives me information that is simply not true. I can never be sure about what I'm hearing, and experience has taught me to accept nothing she says until I check it out independently.

She sounds like someone I should terminate relations with, but I don't. I continue to work with her from time to time because she happens to be a competent dealer and she happens to buy and sell interesting and worthwhile art.

Aside from the fact that I can accept nothing she tells me at face value, she's·great. If I am interested in a work of art she has for sale, I find out the price and that's it. I listen to everything else she says—I don't want to be rude—but then I do the necessary research entirely on my own.

Unfortunately, if you were to meet this dealer for the first time, you would have no idea what to believe and what not to believe. She is entertaining and knowledgeable, and she speaks with great conviction and always sounds sincere. Other art dealers won't warn you about her—you have to learn yourself (dealers rarely gossip in public about fellow dealers). If you buy art based on her advice alone, you might end up with a great piece of art at a fair price, but you might also grossly overpay for a real loser. She makes everything she sells sound equally appetizing.

A LOOK AHEAD

Now that you've had an introduction to art people, you're ready to go out and meet some of them—particularly those that are involved with types of art that relate to your collecting interests. The majority of these people happen to be art dealers, and you will meet them as you shop from gallery to gallery comparing the selections they have to offer.

As you have seen, the more people you meet, the more you can learn about art and the better balanced your art education becomes. In the same vein, the more galleries you visit, the better able you are to select just the right art for your collection and the better balanced your art collection becomes. Naturally, you need instruction in how to locate as many of the right galleries and meet as many of the right dealers as possible, and these topics are covered in the next chapter.

CHAPTER 5

Comparison Shopping for Art

Knowing what you want to collect and being able to select just the right pieces for your collection do not necessarily go hand in hand. So far, you have seen art you like at certain galleries, museums, and other public places, but you have only seen that art as a result of random exposures, not organized, systematic visits. What you have seen to this point is only the beginning.

Shopping for art is like shopping for anything else. Now that you have defined your likes, you need to find out who sells that type of art, speak with them, see what they have to offer, and make gallery-to-gallery comparisons. You have to survey what's available in the marketplace. In order to select worthwhile works of art—ones that are priced fairly and that you won't get tired of looking at—you've got to stifle every impulse to buy immediately and instead make it a point to comparison shop.

Think about how gallery owners select their art. Out of all the millions of art pieces available for sale, they have to decide what to show, which artists to exhibit. Passion and feeling, of course, play significant roles in their selection processes, but there's more. When they see art they like, they research it, evaluate its quality, see what else is available in that category, compare prices, and ultimately determine whether they can remain competitive with other galleries by buying and then selling it. They comparison shop for the art they are best able to sell. Shouldn't you?

WHY EVERYONE DOESN'T COMPARISON SHOP

Many beginning collectors make the mistake of buying art without comparison shopping. They do so primarily because of a misconception they have that I call the "uniqueness myth." They believe that since every work of art is "unique"—one-of-a-kind—they might as well buy what they like when they see it because they'll never find anything else exactly like it.

This myth is only partially true. Any original work of art is unique in the sense that no other work of art looks *exactly* like it, but that's about as far as you can go with this line of reasoning. In spite of its "uniqueness," that work of art also happens to be similar to plenty of other works of art. Let's say, for example, that you see a painting of a Paris street scene. Even though no other Paris street scene painting is a precise duplicate of the one you saw, hundreds of artists have produced countless thousands of Paris street scenes over the years, and if you take the time to look, you can find a number of street scenes that are similar to that one particular scene.

Whatever works of art specifically attract you, you can *always* find a number of other pieces out there that look approximately (and often remarkably) the same. The more art you see, the more you will realize how true this is.

Related to the uniqueness myth is another reason why beginners tend not to comparison shop: they mistake initial attraction for everlasting love. They believe in love at first sight; they believe that they can find "perfect" art, that no other art can provide them with as much satisfaction and enjoyment. This is equivalent to a man who has never been married believing that he will one day meet the perfect partner, recognize her instantly, marry her on the spot, and that the two of them will live happily ever after.

Whenever you see art that attracts you, know that you are being attracted only in the moment, that you are experiencing the love-at-first-sight phenomenon. For this reason, you should avoid the impulse to buy and instead should test that attraction by comparison shopping. Compare the art to similar pieces at other galleries; compare it to totally different pieces at other galleries. You may find art that attracts you just as much, and you may find art that attracts you more. You'll discover this once you begin looking.

Lastly, some collectors don't comparison shop because the galleries they patronize discourage comparison shopping. These establishments don't want their clients to know that worthwhile art can also be found elsewhere. They manipulate clients by saying things like, "Buy this now because you'll never find another one like it," or "This is the best one you'll ever see." They use the "uniqueness myth," the love-at-first-sight phenomenon, and whatever else they have at their disposal in order to keep you inside their galleries and sell you art. These sellers prefer buyers who ask few questions, blindly accept what they are told, and are convinced that the best art can only be found at certain galleries (theirs in particular). We're getting a little ahead of ourselves, though. You'll read more about these sorts of tactics in Chapter 6, "Dealer Dealings" and Chapter 9, "How Not to Buy Art."

ESTABLISHED VERSUS OFFBEAT RESOURCES

The number-one rule to follow when learning how to comparison shop for your selections is this: *Stick with established galleries when you're just starting out.* You need all the protection you can get at this early stage, and you will see in the next chapter why established galleries are simply the best and safest places to begin buying art.

Beating the bushes for art, as so many collectors love to do, can be hazardous to your wallet. Avoid art liquidations, estate sales, yard sales, flea markets, and auctions. Stay away from secondhand stores, places that sell art on the side but really specialize in other merchandise, and so on. Don't shop out of newspaper classifieds or at the homes of private collectors. These are all high-risk ventures, and you need plenty of experience in buying art before you start to shop wherever you happen to see art for sale.

LOCATING GALLERIES THAT SELL WHAT YOU WANT

Comparison shopping for art does not mean that you have to spend months contacting galleries and meeting dealers around the world. Your search depends upon the type of art you have chosen to collect. For example, if you want to buy art by local artists who are active only in your area, you certainly don't have to make national or worldwide efforts to find out who sells it.

As for how exhaustive or comprehensive you want to make your search, that's up to you. You can go out and locate every gallery that sells your type of art, or you can approach the assignment more casually and locate only a few. Know, however, that the amount of effort you put in is directly proportional to the amount of knowledge you will accumulate about your art and about the marketplace for that art, and to the quality of the selections you will eventually make. In any event, do whatever feels most comfortable. A variety of gallery-locating techniques are listed here. Choose and follow whichever ones are applicable to your particular situation.

A good place to begin any art gallery search is by looking at advertisements in major national or international art magazines and newspapers. See Appendix 1 for a partial listing of major art-related periodicals and brief comments about each. Many city, state, and regional art-related periodicals are also available. Check with local art galleries or public libraries to see whether any are published in your area. These periodicals often contain extensive gallery advertisements and provide the best coverage of local and regional art scenes.

Most art-related newspapers and magazines are available at main branches of major public libraries. Libraries that don't shelve them can often borrow them for you from other libraries or tell you where to find them. If spending time in libraries doesn't suit you, you can find most of these periodicals at major bookstores and magazine stores.

Focus your attention primarily on art gallery advertisements. The articles won't help you all that much at this early stage, but if you happen to see one that catches your eye, either read it or note what magazine it appears in and save it for later. The articles are much more helpful after you know your way around the art business a little better.

Some periodicals will appeal to you more than others. Your best tactic is to sample them all at first and eventually subscribe to the ones you enjoy the most and find most helpful to your collecting. In the meantime, browse thoroughly.

If you are interested in art from foreign countries, locate and study a copy of the *International Directory of Arts*. This annual publication is a worldwide guide to museums, art-related institutions, dealers, galleries, and much more. You can find it at most major libraries. (*International Directory of Arts* is published by Art Address Verlag in Frankfurt, Germany. The 1989–90 edition is 1,800 pages in two volumes.)

Here are several additional resources for locating galleries:

- Your local Yellow Pages and those of nearby major cities, under the heading "Art Galleries, Dealers & Consultants."

- Entertainment sections of local newspapers and city, state, or regional general-interest magazines. These often contain gallery advertisements, notices of art openings and ongoing shows, listings of art-related events, and so on. Look for special sections where art galleries list current offerings or exhibits.

- Membership lists of regional, national, and international art-dealer organizations. The major national and international organizations can be found in the *International Directory of Arts* and also in the annual directories published by *Art & Auction* and *Art in America* magazines (see Appendices 2 and 5). Check local galleries and regional art publications for names and addresses of city, state, and regional gallery associations.

- Referrals from collectors, museum curators, and other knowledgeable individuals. Referrals from museum curators and other unbiased professionals are especially helpful. You may not know many experts or authorities yet, but the more involved you become with collecting, the more of these people you'll be introduced to. Much of your most valuable information will eventually come by word of mouth.

As You Research, Make a Working List of All the Galleries You Come Across That Seem to Offer Art or Artists Similar to What You are Interested In. Write down full names, addresses, and phone numbers, and include any other pertinant details, such as where you read the ads, why the ads attracted you, who referred you, and so on. Include the following types of galleries on your list:

- Galleries that sell particular artists whose work you have already seen and like

- Galleries that offer the look you like by whatever artists happen to be producing it, whether you recognize their names or not

- Galleries that offer art you like the looks of, even though you may be totally unfamiliar with it

- Galleries that sell art you like in your price range

- Galleries selling what you like that have been in business for long periods of time

Next, Contact These Galleries. The three ways you can reach them are by phone, letter, or personal visit. Tell everyone you meet where or how you heard about them and what attracted you, and ask for promotional information about the various galleries. Your primary objective here is to view the art for sale by the galleries, either personally or in brochures, and see how much you like it. If you happen to see a selection of art you really like, get basic facts about it and nothing more—the in-depth research and decisions about whether or not to buy come later.

With first contacts like these, keep interactions simple, find out what each gallery sells, and get an idea of whether it's right for you. Don't get involved in long discussions about art. Don't let anyone start selling to you. If you prefer making contacts by phone or mail, don't let anyone pressure you to come in for personal visits—ask the gallery representative to send you any promotional material available on the gallery's art, and that's that. Personal visits are best, however. As soon as possible, visit all galleries that appear to have what you want.

If you're curious about how much a particular work of art costs and the asking price is not readily apparent, ask. This is a good time to begin getting a basic feel for prices. Don't immediately eliminate a gallery if a price quote is way over your budget. The gallery may also sell art with a comparable look and feel that is more in your price range. Keep price discussions simple, though. Advise gallery personnel that you are just beginning your art quest and that you are curious about what sells for how much but don't want to get much more involved than that.

Comparison shopping for art is the process that exposes you to a variety of dealers, a variety of galleries, and a variety of ways of doing business. It gives you an overall understanding of how the marketplace operates and what it has to offer. Comparison shopping provides you with ample opportunities to make intelligent selections for your collection.

You may never do business with many of the galleries you locate and visit. You may decide to buy your art from only two or three or four after all is said and done. No matter how many dealers you eventually patronize, at least you will have made the contacts and had the experiences of meeting them and seeing their places of business. All this gives you a significant advantage over other collectors who never bother to broaden their horizons beyond one or two dealers.

Example 1: The best-quality art is the hardest to find; plenty of collectors are looking for it. When a desirable work of art comes onto the market, many collectors may want to own it, but only one lucky person ends up with it. The collector who does is usually a serious comparison shopper—one who keeps constant contact with a wide range of galleries. Good art sells fast, and the collector who takes the prize home has to be first in line when it arrives at a gallery.

One very thorough collector I know maintains constant contact with many galleries. He stays on top of the market by sending out periodic want lists of the art and artists he is looking for to all dealers whom he thinks could possibly come across pieces that might interest him. When new dealers open their galleries, his list is one of the first things to arrive in their mail. He follows every list with a phone call or a personal visit when possible, introduces himself to the gallery owner, and clearly restates what he is looking for. He is able to point out a number of fine examples in his collection that he has acquired as a result of his diligence.

Example 2: You can actually save money on art by comparison shopping, keeping a wide range of contacts, and knowing many dealers who sell what you like. A significant amount of art is bought, sold, and traded between dealers before it ends up in private collections. One reason for these gallery-to-gallery trans-actions is that dealers are constantly on the lookout for art they know their customers will buy. Dealers scour the market and buy this art wherever they happen to find it, and such an approach includes buying from other galleries.

Let's say that Dealer A knows what you collect. He sees a good example of that art at Dealer B's gallery, a gallery you have never visited. Depending on how sure Dealer A is that you will buy the art, he either buys it outright, trades for it, or asks to have it on consignment so that he can offer it to you.

When Dealer A gets the art from Dealer B he will, in the great majority of cases, raise the price and offer it to you for more than Dealer B is selling it for. If you buy the art from Dealer A, you pay that difference in price for never having met Dealer B. If Dealer B had already known you and was aware of your collecting interests, she would have offered you the art before passing it on to Dealer A. Thus, you could have paid Dealer B's cheaper asking price rather than Dealer A's more expensive one.

In this example, the art passed through only two dealers before it was offered to you. Sometimes art passes through four, five, or even more dealers before it finally ends up in private collections. And the more dealers that handle an art piece before it reaches its final destination, the more expensive it gets. Each dealer adds on a profit margin in the form of a percentage markup, a commission, or a brokering fee. If you keep that dealer-to-dealer chain short, you can save money.

A LOOK AHEAD

The first stages of comparison shopping involve your locating selections you like and cataloguing the best possible resources for return visits. Initial con-tacts are brief, but as you move closer and closer to buying art, interactions become increasingly complex and involved. For these more serious encoun-ters, you need basic information about art dealers and art galleries, the similarities or differences you will find between one gallery and the next, and how to interpret those findings. This information, which is discussed in the next chapter, will protect you from advantage-takers and help you make the most of your gallery contacts.

CHAPTER 6

Dealer Dealings

Art dealers and art galleries are a fact of the art business. The art business cannot exist without them. You have to shop their establishments, and you have to interact, communicate, and negotiate with them at various points in the process of collecting art.

Unfortunately, some art buyers, especially those who are not that knowledgeable about the art business, believe that dealers are a necessary inconvenience that must be tolerated and that all dealers do is buy art cheaply, mark the price way up, stick it in their galleries, and sell it expensively. To them, dealers are nothing more than merchants who are always wanting their piece of the action, mechanically acting as the middleman between one owner and another.

The truth: Art dealers are experts at what they do. Art dealers are professionals that are eminently qualified to handle art in the marketplace. They know how to properly transfer art from artists or private sellers to art collectors and then transfer it again if those collectors ever decide to resell it. Without them, collecting art in any organized manner would be extremely difficult. The art-buying public would have no one to supply them, no one to give them advice, and no formalized settings in which art transactions could take place.

In many ways, art dealers are similar to stockbrokers, real estate agents, and other merchandise brokers. All keep current with their respective markets, know how to place dollar values on what they deal in, know how to locate it and make it available to interested buyers, and are qualified to advise buyers as to what best suits their needs. The best among them spot trends and even dictate tastes.

A word of caution: Art dealers are not gurus to be obeyed without question. As in any business, a few dealers make their livings by taking advantage of unsuspecting clients. Sooner or later you find out who these dealers are and learn to avoid them. The majority of dealers, however, are respected professionals who attend to your particular situation as it relates to the art market in general.

"But buying art from established art dealers and galleries is expensive," you say. "I know what I'm looking for, and I'm going to see whether I can find it elsewhere for less."

Be extremely careful if you're new to the art world and this is what you're thinking. Art is not necessarily cheaper outside of galleries. Yes, prices may seem lower at places like secondhand stores, frame shops, resale outlets, and so on, but look a little closer. What you frequently see are inferior works that art dealers have already passed on or would never consider selling in the first place, not to mention the possibilities of their having condition problems or being outright forgeries.

This is not to say that all art outside of galleries is damaged, inferior, or fake. Quality art *is* out there, but it's tough to find, and plenty of savvy collectors and dealers are after it. What happens all too often, however, is that when amateur art buffs invite art dealers to comment on their backwater bargains, the standard dealer response is, "I hope you can get your money back."

Of course, if you buy from galleries you won't be able to impress your friends with what a super bargain you found at the local secondhand store, nor will you realize instant appreciation on your purchases by paying full gallery retail. But just in case you're interested, the great majority of art gallery art fares *much better* financially over time than does "wherever you happen to find it" art. So in the end you get the most for your money anyway.

"But art is a matter of personal choice," you say. "What I like is my business and no one else's; I don't need art dealers telling me what I should be buying."

Not true. Recognizing quality in art and selecting and eventually buying worthwhile pieces is a learned, not an innate, ability. You must learn what makes art "likable" (good) or "not likable" (bad) in order to make intelligent "personal choices." Art dealers come in mighty handy here for a number of reasons:

- Art dealers see thousands of works of art. All they do is look at art, and when they take a break from looking, they talk about art. Their recommendations come from broad-based knowledge of the art market.

- Art dealers are qualified to give you specialized financial advice about whatever art you are considering buying.

- Art dealers screen all art that is offered to them and resell only the best.

- Art dealers educate you. They answer your questions, explain specific art and artists in depth, recommend books to read, and share other important knowledge. They want you to gain experience.

- The best dealers offer money-back guarantees of authenticity, full condition reports, trade-back arrangements, free updated appraisals, consultations on the scope and direction of your collection, and other amenities. Try getting *those* at the flea market.

Now supposing that some years after you start buying art, you decide to sell some of it. Your tastes have changed, you're moving into smaller quarters, you're upgrading your collection, or whatever. Dealers come in mighty handy in these instances, too. This book is about buying art, not selling it, but nevertheless, you should know at least a little about how dealers help you sell as well as buy.

"But I know how much my art is worth," you say. "I can sell it on my own without any outside help."

Believing this is a big mistake—in fact, it's three big mistakes.

First mistake: Private sellers think that with no professional help they can accurately determine how much their art is worth. The dollar values they come up with are rarely accurate (usually too high) and almost always based on inadequate and arbitrary research. *The facts:* You have to know an artist and his or her market inside and out in order to value art accurately.

Second mistake: Sellers believe they can locate the perfect private collectors for their art. They take out classified ads in newspapers and magazines, they hang out at antique shows or art auctions looking to see who the big buyers are, they read articles about collectors and write them letters, and so on. *The facts:* Contacting private collectors personally is difficult; private collectors prefer to remain private.

Third mistake: Sellers believe they can sell their art to collectors at full retail or, what's even more absurd, to dealers at full retail. *The facts:* Selling to private collectors is harder than finding them. Collectors pay retail to long-established galleries they know and trust. They pay retail for the amenities that galleries provide, and they are not inclined to buy art with no guarantees from total strangers. Dealers, on the other hand, buy at wholesale and sell at retail—they obviously do not buy art at the same price they sell it for, or they wouldn't be in business.

Dealers help you sell your art in ways you can't help yourself. They know the market for your art, they know detailed information about the artists, they know who collects those artists. And there's more:

• Dealers recognize how important your art is, how that art fits into the artist's careers, whether it is high end or low end in terms of quality, and so on.

• Dealers recognize the strengths and weaknesses in your art and the strengths and weaknesses in the markets for that art.

- Dealers know which collectors would like to own your art. They understand the individual needs of those collectors and know how to properly present your art. Dealers stand a much better chance of selling your art to those collectors than you do.

- Dealers give you a realistic idea of how much money you can expect to sell for.

- Dealers often net you more for your art than what you can net by selling to "private collectors" on your own. Believe it or not!

Art dealers are in business to help you whenever your situation involves a transaction in art. Whether you're buying, selling, trading, or collecting, take advantage of the services that dealers offer and the insight they provide.

All is not wonderful in art-dealer-land, however. In a perfect world where everything was fair, buying art would be easy. You could visit any art gallery, present your situation, state what you wanted to buy and how much you wished to spend on it, make your selection, write out the check, and take your new acquisition home with you. Unfortunately, we do not live in a perfect world, and buying art is not quite that straightforward. Not every dealer is fair.

The art business, like any other business, is populated with great dealers, good dealers, average dealers, worse-than-average dealers, and a few terrible dealers. The art they sell ranges, in like fashion, from excellent to awful. Prices range, too. Most are fair and reasonable, but a few are ridiculously inflated. Major goals of your comparison shopping are to meet, understand, and communicate with dealers and, ultimately, to differentiate between who sells good-quality art at the right prices and who doesn't—and who has the best (and worst) selections for you.

CHARACTERISTICS OF GOOD ART DEALERS

Good Dealers Listen to What You Have to Say. They allow you to lead the discussion about what you are interested in collecting. They want to know what you are looking for. They show you any art they have in stock that could possibly interest you. If they don't have anything in your field, they refer you to galleries that do.

Good Dealers Want You to Learn. They determine how much you know, offer advice where it is needed, and suggest where you need help. They either tell you who is qualified to teach you, or they do it themselves.

Good Dealers Discuss Options. They offer you a variety of alternatives as to which direction you can take with your collecting. They discuss the good and bad points of each option. They never make you feel pressured to move in any particular direction.

Good Dealers Give You Plenty of Facts. They discuss the visual, scholarly, aesthetic, and historical aspects of the art you are interested in. They compare and contrast artists, quality levels, works of art, and art prices. All your questions are answered in a direct and straightforward fashion.

Good Dealers Provide You With Outside Tools and Resources for Continuing Your Education On Your Own. They recommend books to read, museums to visit, experts and collectors to meet, collections to see. They present you with information not only from their own galleries but also from other galleries. They do not try to convince you that their galleries are the only ones you should ever patronize.

Good Dealers Speak Your Language and Work With You at Your Own Pace. You never feel compelled to buy. You are always free to make your own decisions. You leave their galleries knowing more than when you arrive, and you feel that they are genuinely concerned about your success as a collector.

DEALERS TO WATCH OUT FOR

Unfortunately, not all art dealers have your best interests in mind when they attempt to sell you art. These dealers can be avoided, though. Certain telltale signs almost always mean you should exit the gallery you're in and move on to another.

Avoid Dealers Whose Sales Presentations Focus Primarily On the Emotional. These dealers speak only about the way the art looks—the beauty, the drama, the color, the intensity, the feeling. If you listen carefully, however, you notice that important details are conspicuously absent from the presentation, namely facts about the art, the artist, and the market for the art.

Watch Out for Dealers Who Avoid Price Talk. They're usually evasive for a reason, most likely because what they sell is overpriced and they prefer not talking about it. They would rather haul you into their private viewing rooms and tell you how their art transports you into unique and pleasant worlds (the financial world not being one of them). Interrupt the travelogue with price questions, and you can get some rather strange and occasionally ugly responses. Any time you hear things like, "If you have to ask the price

. . . ," or "It's worth many times that in beauty alone," or "How you feel is what's important, not how much it costs," you're in trouble.

Dealers, of course, have a right to say whatever they want about the price of the art they sell. No law forbids them from believing that price is irrelevant and what counts is the mystic, cosmic interplay between you and the essense of the artist as embodied in the art. But the facts are that any art piece has a corresponding fair and reasonable dollar value, one that anyone familiar with that artist's market will agree on, give or take a little.

Watch Out for Dealers Who Focus Their Sales Presentations Only On Money. These are the exact opposite of those who avoid price talk. All these dealers do is talk money. The worst offenders go so far as to totally ignore the way the art looks and sell artwork as if it were stocks or bonds. In the extreme instance, galleries tell prospective clients that they will enjoy set percentages of appreciation over specific time periods—which is a ridiculous, misleading, and borderline fraudulent way of selling art.

In a way, the people who buy art based on financial reasons alone are as much to blame as the dealers for the proliferation of dollar-oriented selling. A good percentage of buyers, especially first-time buyers, are attracted to art by the possibilities of financial gain, and such buyers make easy marks for investment-style selling. Dealers simply play into their fantasies about buying art now for big profits later.

Typical statements you hear during the course of a make-big-bucks-fast sales presentation are:

"Who cares whether or not you like it. In eighteen months it'll be worth twice what you're paying for it."

"As soon as this artist has a show at the Municipal Art Museum, you won't be able to touch one for this price."

"Buy one while you can still afford it."

"This artist isn't going to be around for much longer. As soon as he dies, his prices are going through the roof."

"This edition is almost sold out. Cash in while we still have some left. Once it sells out, prices will double."

"This is the only one of its kind. Buy now or forget about ever being able to buy one as good for as little money again."

"This piece will make a great investment."

"You could buy these for a song ten years ago. Think what they'll be worth ten years from now."

These statements are not only untrue, they're also disgusting. To portray a piece of art as nothing more than a speculative commodity, or an artist as a person who will hopefully die soon and boost the value of his own art is the basest way to operate an art business. Anytime you find yourself in these sorts of situations, no matter how much money you are being told you can make, leave immediately.

Watch Out for Dealers Who Attempt to Qualify You as a Buyer. They decide how much of their time is worth spending on you based on the amount of money you have to spend with them.

One gallery I know of that specializes in selling overpriced art to unsuspecting out-of-town buyers has a calculated way to get to the bottom line. When you visit this gallery, shortly after your entrance a sales person asks you the question, "Are you in town attending the medical convention?" A medical convention may or may not be taking place, but that's irrelevant. The question is a lead-in to finding out what you do for a living and, therefore, whether or not you can afford this gallery's art. If you answer no, the staff person responds with "I thought for sure you were a doctor. You certainly look like one. What do you do for a living?" or "What brings you to the city then?" or "I've been seeing doctors all week, and I'm ready for a change. What do you do for a living?" If you answer the question and your occupation implies that you have money, get ready for an aggressive sales presentation.

Avoid Dealers Who are Not Sensitive to Your Needs and Who Don't Listen to You. With such dealers you are usually forced to look at art you are not the least bit interested in. Rather than admitting that they don't sell what you want and referring you to galleries that do, these dealers try to change your mind and force you to buy what they sell.

Watch Out for Dealers Who Focus On One or Two Artists, Ones They Represent or Have Good Stocks of, and Avoid All Others. No matter what you say, the conversation always returns to these several artists. You get a very one-sided picture of the art market from these dealers. Avoid them unless, of course, they happen to be dealing in artists you collect.

Avoid Dealers Who Pressure You, Who Need Your Sale to Make Their Next Commission, and Who Are Constantly On Top of You to Buy. Being victimized by a hard sell is always painful. Galleries that are more concerned about their bottom line than serving your needs are a sad fact of the art business. When you feel that the art wants you rather than that you want the art, "just say no."

Watch Out for Dealers Who Find Out How Little You Know About Certain Art or Artists and Then Go to Work Educating You Whether You Want to Learn or Not. Once such dealers see you're not experienced, anything goes. You may be introduced to a "world famous" painter, one that a seller can't believe you've never heard of. You may get spoken to in "secret technical art lingo" that you don't understand but that you can have the privilege of learning if you decide to patronize that gallery. Never let anyone bully you with supposed expertise.

Finally, Avoid Art Dealers Who Answer Any of Your Questions About Their Art With the Reply "I Don't Know." This answer is *never* acceptable, no matter what the question. At the very least, it's an indication that the dealer is uninformed about some aspect of what he or she is selling. It's also a convenient way of dodging a touchy question, such as whether the art is worth what you are being asked to pay for it. At worst, "I don't know" is a great way for a dealer to avoid telling you something he or she doesn't want *you* to know.

Example 1: Antique dealers occasionally call me when they meet private individuals who have art for sale. One time, an out-of-town dealer called to tell me about a middle-aged couple who had a group of paintings for sale and asked me to come out and take a look. I wanted to make sure the trip would be worth my while, so I asked him to find out some particulars about the art and call me back.

The next day he called to tell me that the paintings had originally come from an elderly lady who had apparently acquired them over a twenty- or thirty-year period. He then gave me basic information about some of the paintings concerning sizes, subject matters, artists' names, and how much the couple was asking for them. Several of the artists were collectible, and all the asking prices were reasonable. What I heard sounded good, so I decided to make the trip.

I arrived at the couple's home and introduced myself. The husband led me into a rear room and, with a sweep of his hand, directed my attention toward the paintings, all of which were leaning against a wall and stacked one in front of the other. I began looking through them and immediately realized that this trip was going to be a complete waste of time.

The paintings by name artists were either outright forgeries or terrible examples. The rest were by complete unknowns. I had even seen some of these paintings for sale at various shops over the past several years, which meant that, on top of everything else, the "elderly lady" story was a lie.

I looked through the collection, bought nothing, politely thanked the couple for their time, and left. The sad part of this story is that several weeks later I was at the home of a relatively inexperienced collector who proudly told me he had beat the dealers and made a great art buy out of a private home. He showed me his three latest acquisitions and—you guessed it—they had all come from this out-of-town couple. One of the paintings was a forgery that he had paid almost $2,000 for. The other two were junk.

Example 2: Some collectors prefer buying their art directly from the artists to buying it from dealers. They enjoy meeting the artists in person in their studios and negotiating purchases without dealer interference. This is fine, but once again, be aware that if you buy without dealer assistance, you'd better know what you're doing first. There are drawbacks to buying directly from the artist.

First of all, artists are not art dealers (with a few exceptions), and artists' studios are not art galleries. Artists are experts at creating art, not selling it. Most are far removed from the business of buying and selling art.

Artists do not stay on top of current events in the art business. They do not provide amenities that galleries do, such as trade-back policies or free updated appraisals. They cannot provide you with an overview of the market the way that dealers can.

Artists focus primarily on their own work. They often give you very biased ideas about what your buying options are. You would not, for instance, expect an artist to suggest that her work is not right for you and then refer you to another artist whose work she thinks would better suit your tastes. According to her, her work is what suits you, and that's that. (Of course, not all artists fit these generalizations.)

As for you, arbitrarily picking artists whose work you happen to like is not the best way to collect. Until you acquire a good overview of the market, you'll have difficulty recognizing which artists to collect, whether or not to pay their asking prices, whether you are getting the best-quality work for your money, and so on. Have dealers help you make those sorts of decisions while you're still in the learning stages. Then, once you've developed a feel for what you're doing, buying from artists can be a very rewarding experience.

A LOOK AHEAD

Being able to distinguish between one art dealer and the next is a big step toward selecting the right art, but it's only part of what you need to know.

Dealers operate and sell art from their galleries, places where you will be spending significant amounts of time viewing art, learning about art, and eventually buying art. Understanding what art galleries are and knowing how to use them to their full potential is just as important as understanding the dealers who operate them, and Chapter 7 will help you with this aspect of buying art.

CHAPTER 7
What to Do Inside Art Galleries

When you step into an art gallery, you encounter much more than an art dealer standing in a room full of art. You leave the everyday world behind and enter a unique microcosm of reality. The term *art gallery* is almost too mild a description of what confronts you once you are inside. Most galleries could more accurately be described as shrines to art, or art temples. They are places where art is hallowed above all else and where devotion to that art is embodied in the ceremony of dealers passing it on to collectors in exchange for money.

Galleries are designed to focus your total attention on the particular art or artists they represent. When they do their job well, you are aware only of what's going on right before your eyes. Your life, for those brief moments, consists of art, art, and art.

Whenever you're inside a gallery that displays art you find appealing, you feel compelled to a certain extent to select a piece or two for your collection. A portion of that compulsion may be attributed to your genuine desire to own the art and another portion to the gallery's efforts to convince or induce you to own it. Some of the more intimidating galleries can actually interfere with and alter your normal decision-making process in favor of their art.

Controlling your own destiny inside galleries is not always easy. Meeting art dealers on their home turf can be difficult, especially for beginning collectors. The dealers and their staffs know plenty; you hardly know anything. They have dealt with thousands of customers; you've barely had a chance to get your feet wet. They have all their sales tools right there at their fingertips; you have nothing. They see certain qualities in you the moment you walk through their doors; you don't have vaguest idea of what these galleries are about and what to expect from them. They have all the advantages.

This is not to say that art dealers lie in wait in their galleries, ready to play on your inexperience and manipulate the way you think. Most don't. But they *are* interested in selling their art, and if they can figure out how to talk you into buying some, they'll do so. In order to buy art smart, you have to know how to navigate your way through art galleries; understand what happens within them; and know what to look for, what to watch out for, and how to interpret it all.

53

GALLERY INTERIORS VERSUS THE REST OF THE WORLD

Art gallery interiors present art at its absolute highest level of appeal. The track lighting is perfectly focused, the walls behind the art are plain, the carpet or flooring is simple. You see little, if any, competition from the surrounding environment. These are important points to keep in mind, because under such circumstances, just about anything looks great. When properly displayed and lit, a sack full of trash can look like a masterpiece worthy of a place in any of the world's great art museums.

Other fixtures of gallery interiors are the gallery owners and staff. The information they present you with is designed to heighten the beauty of their art even further. They believe in what they sell, and they know exactly what to say in order to sell it.

Finally, you have the art gallery viewing room, the place where art looks even better than it does in any other location on the gallery floor. Galleries without viewing rooms have special spots where their art looks best. When you and an owner or staff person head over to the viewing room or viewing spot, art in tow, for a closer look under these perfectly ideal viewing conditions, you see that art at its absolute unobstructed finest. At this point, you have to be completely sure whether you want to own it or not, because the deck is definitely stacked in the gallery's favor.

Keep in mind that if you buy the art, you have to remove it from the protective environment of the gallery and take it out into the cold, cruel world where it is no longer the center of the universe and no longer has a supporting cast telling you how great it is. It gets no special treatment in your environment; it becomes just another thing in a room full of things. Suddenly, it has to stand on its own and prove that it is really as great as the gallery made it look and made you think it is. The truth is that sometimes it is, and other times it isn't.

Many inexperienced collectors, unfortunately, do not account for the effects that ideal viewing conditions of art gallery interiors combined with overwhelmingly positive employee input can have on art. They buy art on the spot without ever seeing it outside gallery settings and away from the hype, display it in totally different settings, and expect it to thrill them just as much as it did at the galleries. Several weeks or months later, they begin to wonder why it doesn't look as great as they originally thought it did when they bought it. At worst, they actually regret buying it.

What you have to do to prevent this from happening to you is to take any selections you are considering buying out of the viewing rooms, out of the galleries, away from the sales people, and into your own environment—and keep them there for a few days—*before you buy them.* You see and hear how great they are from the sellers. Now you must let gallery influences fade into the background, let your personal feelings come to the foreground, and decide whether or not the art really means as much to you as the gallery presentation lead you to believe it does.

How do you take a selection out of a gallery without having to buy it? Easy. Art galleries offer a courtesy, known as *"taking art home on approval,"* that allows you to keep art, at no financial risk, for anywhere from several days to a week for the sole purpose of deciding whether or not you are sure you want to own it. Some galleries ask you to leave deposits or even pay for the art in full when you do this, but all will completely refund your money if for any reason you decide not to buy.

When you're just starting out in your collecting, always take art you have selected for possible purchase home with you on approval first. You will see for yourself how drastically gallery interiors and sales presentations can sometimes influence the way art looks, and you will discover that some art you initially thought you wanted to buy is really not for you at all.

ART GALLERY BACK ROOMS, STORAGE AREAS, AND OFFICES

Almost all art galleries have more art for sale than what you see on display in the public viewing areas. Galleries often have additional art stored in stock rooms, back rooms, office areas, separate warehouse storage facilities, and so on. Some galleries keep photo albums of art that they have in storage, pieces they have access to out of private collections, and art they can purchase for you through other dealers. A gallery may have ten additional pieces available, or it may have ten thousand.

Whenever you are in a gallery and don't see art that interests you, never turn around and walk out. Introduce yourself to the owner or a staff person, state exactly what you're looking for, and find out whether the gallery has access to any art for you even though none is currently on display. You do yourself a major disservice everytime you browse in silence and then leave, because you miss seeing everything for sale that is out of public view.

See back-room selections and actually go into storage areas with dealers whenever possible. These experiences add to your knowledge of how galleries operate and to your understanding of the range and variety of art that galleries have to offer. Other advantages to seeing art in storage are as follows:

- A gallery may have large holdings in an artist or type of art that you like but may not currently be showing it.

- A gallery may have large holdings in an artist that you are not familiar with but whose art you find appealing once you have a chance to see numerous examples.

- You may notice art you like that gallery owners forgot they even had for sale.

- You may find art you like that is out of place in a particular gallery and that the owner is willing to let you have at an attractive price.

- You are afforded opportunities to learn about art and artists whose work gallery owners keep in stock but never display in public areas.

- Dealers understand from how you respond to the full scope of their art how best they will be able to help you in the future.

As with storage areas, offices can be interesting and informative, so whenever you have the opportunity to see and speak with gallery owners and staff people in their offices, do so. Visiting office areas and seeing the centers of operations increases your understanding of what art galleries are all about and makes you less intimidated and thus better able to make decisions regarding the substance and direction of your collecting.

Another advantage to office access and access to places other than the main floor is that you get the chance to see new arrivals and hear about the latest developments before the general public does. When things happen, they happen in offices and back rooms first. Acquiring this sort of inside access takes time and is part of the process of developing long-term working relationships with dealers, but as you get to know certain dealers better, you'll find yourself receiving special attention that ordinary clients do not normally receive.

ART GALLERY LIBRARIES

In any gallery, pay attention to all books, exhibition catalogues, and other art reference materials out on display for public use. Even more important than that, though, look for the gallery art library. A gallery library may consist of five books, or it may consist of five thousand. It may be in an office, in a work or storage room, or out on the main floor. Libraries are usually in plain sight, but when you can't find one, ask whether one exists and, if it does, whether you can see it.

An art gallery library contains art books, exhibition catalogues, art periodicals, and other materials that relate to what the gallery sells. Art dealers use these reference materials when they have to research particular artists or works of art. A comprehensive library is indispensable to a good art dealer and is an excellent indication of how serious that gallery is about knowing the history and details behind the art it sells and having the means on hand of conveying that information to their customers.

Good reference libraries should contain standard references like those you will learn about in Part III. The more of those you see, the better. Also, the more a gallery refers to them and shares that information with you, the better. The best galleries support any claims they make about their art with substantial documentation from standard reference materials that are recognized and accepted by those in the art community.

Better gallery libraries also contain substantial price reference materials which you will learn about in Part IV. Briefly, the more standard and widely accepted price references you see, the more galleries refer to them; and the more they share that information with you, the better.

Get into the habit of asking gallery owners or staff people whether they can provide you with printed information about particular art or artists they have on display that you are interested in. Make them use their libraries. This gives you the chance to see how they do research and also allows you to learn what books and catalogues provide the best answers to your specific questions. Most dealers are experts at art research; learn from them whenever you get the chance.

One caution, though. Ask for library references only when you're seriously considering the art. Avoid making frivolous requests and forcing dealers to haul out book after book when you're not really interested in learning about or buying the art you're asking questions about.

Beware of galleries that have no libraries to speak of. Galleries with minimal reference materials on hand are often more interested in merchandising art than in educating and cultivating informed collectors. A poor or nonexistent gallery reference library is never a good sign.

TIPS ON RECOGNIZING THE BEST (AND WORST) GALLERIES FOR YOU

The goal of all gallery visits is to identify those establishments best able to supply you with the art you want to collect. As you progress from brief initial contacts to in-depth interactions, you will be choosing those places that you will most likely be doing business with in the future. Here are the two most important characteristics you want those galleries to have:

- Wide selections in particular artists or types of art that you find appealing

- Personnel who have a wide range of knowledge about that art, have substantial experience selling it, and show a sensitivity to your collecting needs.

Galleries that do not meet the two conditions, on the other hand, are not good places for beginners to shop.

Avoid Establishments That Offer Only Isolated Examples of Art You Like; Avoid Gallery Personnel Who Are Not Informed About It. While you're in the learning stages, you need to surround yourself with experts. You take serious risks if you don't.

Suppose, for example, you walk into a gallery because you see an attractive bronze statue by a sculptor whose work you like on display in the front window. You take a look around and see no other work by this artist. You ask the owner about the sculpture, and during the course of conversation you find out that it's the only work by this sculptor that he has ever had for sale, that he has learned most of what he's telling you only since he acquired it, and that he has only seen several other pieces by the artist during his entire career. Conclusion: This dealer does not qualify as an authority on the sculptor, and, unless you are an authority, you would be ill advised to buy the sculpture.

Avoid Galleries That Have No Direction or Focus in What They Sell. These places are easy to spot because they display many unrelated pieces of art by many different artists, spanning many time periods, styles, and so on. When the selection gets too general, the amount of knowledge the dealer has about that selection is usually too general also.

Example 1: A collector once came to me with a "bargain" painting he had discovered while rummaging through the back-room stock of a local art gallery. He said the dealer appeared to know a little about the artist but was not that familiar with his market and how desirable his art was. That was why the price was so low.

I took one look at it and saw that it was a fake—a good fake, but a fake nonetheless. I recommended that he return it as soon as possible, but just to be on the safe side, I had him contact another dealer first in order to confirm my suspicions. The dealer agreed with my assessment, and the collector returned the picture to the gallery and, fortunately, was able to get his money back without any problem.

What happened here was that this collector was not yet experienced enough to be buying odd works of art out of dealer back rooms. He knew that this particular artist was highly collectible and had seen a few examples of the artist's work, but that was about all. He automatically took the word of the dealer (who didn't know enough about the artist either), and he ended up getting fooled by a good-quality forgery.

A big problem with dealers who are not experts in what they sell is that they can inadvertently buy and sell forgeries. These dealers think they are buying and selling authentic art, but in some cases they do not know enough to tell the difference between the real thing and skillfully executed fakes.

Example 2: A collector once asked me about a sculptor whose work he was interested in purchasing. He had visited a gallery where he had seen the artist's work for the first time and liked it very much. The gallery owner had fueled this collector's enthusiasm by showing him a book that contained an entire chapter on the sculptor. The collector believed from this presentation that the artist was extremely well known and almost famous.

I was familiar with this artist and told the collector that he had been given the wrong impression. Although the artist was known and respected, the artist's being categorized as "extremely well known" or "almost famous" was definitely out of the question. Seeing that much of his excitement seemed to be based on the one chapter that had been written about the artist, I asked what book the dealer had showed him.

He gave me the name of the book and I immediately recognized it as an insignificant reference. True, the sculptor did have a chapter in the book, but the artists included were not included because they were famous. They were included primarily because they had been friends of the author. The book contained little scholarly information but was rather a collection of anecdotes about how various artists lived their lives.

Dealers occasionally abuse their libraries when documenting the art they sell. By showing only selected references, they attempt to inflate the reputations of their artists in order to justify unreasonable asking prices. Read everything dealers show you, but unless you know and trust the dealers, never assume that they're giving you either a balanced presentation or all the information you need to know.

A LOOK AHEAD

Understanding art dealers and art galleries well enough to choose the best ones for your needs is essential to intelligent collecting. You do not, however, simply decide who you're going to buy from, sit back, and wait for the art to roll in. In order to assure yourself of getting the best treatment possible in the marketplace and of being shown the greatest number of selections relating to your requirements, you have to know how to be a good customer. Some tips on being a good customer are presented in the next chapter.

CHAPTER 8

How to Be a Good Customer

A dealer–customer relationship is a cooperative venture. You each have obligations to fulfill in order to make it work. Dealers supply you with art, educate you about that art, and, through their galleries, provide amenities, guarantees, and protections on the art you buy. Throughout this process of locating and selling you art, dealers prefer that you cooperate with them and follow certain guidelines. By doing so, you make their job of serving you much easier.

In general, dealers like doing business with collectors who are serious about art and willing to learn. They offer these clients many fringe benefits that average buyers never receive, such as showing them newly arriving art first. These sorts of arrangements do not develop overnight—some relationships can take months or even years to mature—but once they do, collecting becomes less of an effort and even more of a pleasure.

THINGS DEALERS LIKE

About the Most Important Favor You Can Do for Dealers is to Learn What They Ask You to Learn. The better you understand the language and the history behind what you collect, the better you are able to communicate your needs. Informed, educated buyers are easy to work with—it's that simple. Observe the additional directives listed in this section to hasten your attainment of "most favored collector" status among dealers.

Always Be as Specific as Possible about What Type of Art You are Looking For. Specify that you are seeking nineteenth-century paintings of horses by English artists, contemporary watercolor scenes of the Mississippi River Valley, sculptures done by Brazilian artists since the 1940s, limited edition prints of big game animals, or whatever. As you gain experience, you should become progressively more detailed in defining your needs. Tell dealers about your favorite artists, subject matters, colors, sizes, shapes, and any other characteristics you prefer in your art. Also keep them informed as to any changes or new developments in the direction of your collecting.

Respond as Quickly and Directly as Possible to All Art that Dealers Show You. Tell them whether or not you like it and why. Be as precise as you can, and say everything that comes to mind. Don't feel shy or embarrassed—

you learn by speaking with experts. For example, spending half an hour with a dealer evaluating the pluses and minuses of a particular painting can be a highly enlightening and educational exercise.

Know Your Budget, and Never Mislead Anyone About Your Ability to Buy. Be fair with dealers on this issue, and they'll return the favor. For example, if you are in a gallery that has little for sale under $10,000 and you have a limit of $1,500 per acquisition, say so. Nobody's going to throw you out. Most likely, people at the gallery will still be happy to speak with you about their art and artists, and maybe on some future visit you'll be able to afford a piece of their art.

Encourage Dealers to Call You, to Show You Special Considerations, and to Inform You about New Arrivals. You are never under any obligation to buy. Of course, if you don't buy, they'll stop calling you, but by that time you may have settled on other dealers whom you prefer doing business with anyway.

Act Immediately When Dealers Call You about Art They Think You Might Be Interested in, whether You Want it or Not. Dealers appreciate quick responses because then they can either sell you the art or, if you don't want it, proceed to call whoever's next in line. If you make dealers wait for days before you respond, you can bet they won't be calling you back in the future.

Buy Art! Buy art from galleries that offer what you want, both in terms of art, art education, and other amenities. Galleries that take the time to teach you expect something in return. If all you do is take without giving, you'll find that gallery owners will eventually cut communications with you.

Be Loyal to the Dealers that Help You the Most. This does not mean that you blindly buy from one or two dealers and ignore the rest of the art world. Get to know your favorite dealers, visit their galleries regularly, solidify relationships, work together whenever possible, make sure they know how much you appreciate everything they do for you, and generally keep in touch. Continue to meet new dealers at all times and to buy from whoever happens to come up with what you want, but maintain and deepen good relations with those who have been helping you the longest.

Pay for What You Buy When You Say You are Going to Pay for It. Whether you are supposed to pay over several months or within three days, pay on time. Dealers need to know when and how much money is coming into their galleries so that they can gauge their own purchases and pay their bills on time.

Listen to the Advice Dealers Give You, Even When It May Not Be What You Want to Hear. This doesn't mean that you must instantly accept whatever they say, but rather that you show a willingness to consider new input and ideas that may diverge from those you already have. Much of what dealers tell you is for your benefit, and by keeping an open mind, you allow yourself to grow as a collector.

THINGS DEALERS DON'T LIKE

You want dealers to like you. When they don't, you and your collection suffer. Dealers who don't like you behave in ways that are counterproductive to your collection, for example:

- They spend as little time with you as possible.

- They don't educate you.

- They don't care whether they sell you quality art or not.

- They don't inform you about the latest developments in the art market.

- They don't speak favorably of you when your name comes up in conversations with other dealers or collectors.

- They may purposely mislead you.

Observing a few specific cautions, as outlined below, will keep you off of dealers' "least favored clients" lists.

Don't Be a Silent Customer, a Mystery Person. When you visit galleries, introduce yourself, ask questions, and state what you're looking for. No one likes collectors who are cagey or secretive about their intentions.

Don't Constantly Take Information Without Offering Something in Return (in Other Words, Buying Art). Dealers know when they are being hit up for free advice, and they don't like it. You can ask dealers you already do business with for informational favors, but make sure that in the long run you compensate them for their time.

Don't Talk a Big Game About How Much Money You Have to Spend or Are Willing to Spend and Then Not Spend Any. Dealers are not interested in listening to how much money you have either before or after you spend it. By the way, as far as dealers are concerned, you have no money to spend until you spend it.

Avoid Playing Dealers off One Against the Other. Ask dealers to comment on each other's art or tell dealers what other dealers are saying about each other's art, and you'll find yourself in trouble fast.

Don't Be Cheap. If you know that $1,000 is a fair price to pay for the art you want, don't offer $500 for it. First of all, you'll never own any art. Second, you'll waste everyone's time, including your own. Third, you'll get a reputation as a cheap buyer, and those dealers who continue doing business with you will only offer you cheap art—cheap in quality as well as price.

Don't Attempt to Hide Your Enthusiasm About Art You Really Like. Some collectors think that if they remain totally unemotional, show no feelings, and express take-it-or-leave-it attitudes, dealers will drop asking prices and sell for less. First of all, dealers show the greatest consideration to customers who are excited and completely satisfied with what they buy. Second, dealers love to know when they pinpoint tastes exactly. Third, the deadpan routine rarely fools anyone. Start playing sneaky games with dealers and they'll respond with a few of their own.

Avoid Showing Off Good Buys You Make from Other Dealers. If you find a bargain somewhere, great. Suppress the urge to brag about how clever you are. Act like you know so much that you can buy art without dealer assistance, and guess what? Dealers will stop assisting you. Smart collectors savor their bargain buys quietly.

Don't Tell Dealers That You Can Find Art Just As Good As Theirs at Other Galleries for Less Money. Buy art where you get the best quality for the best price and that's that. Going public with gallery-to-gallery price comparisons irritates dealers—and besides that, you probably aren't telling them anything they don't already know.

Don't Respond Rudely to Art That Dealers Offer You. If you don't like the way a piece of art looks, say something like, "It's not quite my style," or "It doesn't have the right feel to it." Go into graphic detail about how your eyes ache when you look at it or complain that it makes you nauseous and you'll lose a dealer's support quickly. Insult the art, and you insult the dealer who is selling it.

Don't Treat Dealers like Servants or Hired Help and Feel That They Should Pay Homage because You Have Graciously Singled Out Their Galleries to Do Business With. Dealers respond to this treatment by either avoiding you altogether or by taking your money and returning as little as possible above and beyond what they sell you. You don't do dealers any favors by buying their art.

Example 1: Gossip is a fact of the art business. The art world is small, and many dealers know each other and often speak among themselves about their clients. If you buy art on a regular basis, sooner or later the dealers who specialize in the art you like find out who you are. Some of them hear about you before they even meet you.

When I meet collectors for the first time, I often ask other dealers about them. I basically want to protect myself from people who could possibly cause me trouble, waste my time, or try to take advantage of me. Dealers warn me when I'm in for a rough time, and on occasion I decide not to do business with certain collectors. In the worst instances, I'm warned about certain collectors ahead of time and, based on the strength of those warnings, decide not to do business with them without ever meeting them!

Dealers also have good things to say about collectors. They talk about collectors who are eager to learn, who pay their bills on time, who know how to recognize quality art, and so on. I look forward to doing business with these people and am inclined to show them special considerations, even when I hardly know them.

Make sure that you treat dealers fairly and with respect, because in the art business your reputation often precedes you. Having dealers hear negative things about you before they know you can do a great deal of harm. On the other hand, when they hear good things about you, you have an automatic head start in building a gratifying working relationship.

Example 2: I know a collector who would rather buy a lot of inexpensive paintings than a few expensive ones. Consequently, he ends up sacrificing quality for quantity. Most of his pictures are so bad that even for what little he spends on them, they're still wastes of money. Unfortunately, he refuses to listen to constructive advice from dealers.

Dealers have long since stopped trying to educate this fellow and instead supply him with exactly what he wants—cheap, bad paintings. They don't waste their time showing him anything that's any good because they know it will always be "over his budget." Remember, most dealers want to see you advance as a collector, so seriously consider any advice they give you about improving your buying habits.

A LOOK AHEAD

You have a basic knowledge, at this point, of how the art business works. You know about art dealers, art galleries, and what your responsibilities are in the dealer–collector relationship. Being able to implement this knowledge can only result in one outcome: your selecting quality works of art for your collection. In order to further guarantee positive results in the marketplace, though, you need some additional general instruction in how *not* to select and buy art—that is, how to avoid common mistakes that far too many beginning collectors make. Chapter 9 will help steer you away from the common pitfalls that snag beginning collectors.

CHAPTER 9
How *Not* to Buy Art

This chapter is about "don'ts." Just as you do follow certain rules and procedures when buying art, you don't follow certain other rules and procedures unless you want to end up regretting the day you ever decided to get involved with art. Some of the don'ts you are about to read might sound almost too obvious to mention, and others are being repeated just to make sure you always remember them. Unfortunately, beginning buyers ignore them all the time and end up selecting art for their collections that they should never have considered in the first place.

The don't list teaches you how *not* to buy art. These don'ts are in no particular order. One is just as important as the next. They concern situations in which you could easily find yourself as you wend your way through the art world. Obey them and you'll get good art for your money; ignore them and there's no telling what you'll end up with.

Don't Buy Art Without Thinking. Ask questions and get the facts about any selections you make before you buy. True, buying art should be fun, spontaneous, passionate, and so on, but that doesn't mean that you take leave of all reasoning capacities and abandon yourself to whimsy, ignorance, or impulse.

Don't Confuse Art With the Environment You See It In. The circumstances, surroundings, and happenings taking place at a gallery are entirely separate from the art the gallery is selling. When you buy art, all you get is art; none of that glitz, glamour, and other fun stuff leaves the gallery with you as you walk out the door with your purchase.

Don't Buy Art While Under the Influence Of Drugs or Alcohol. Alter your consciousness and you impair your ability to judge what's right for you, both in terms of the appearance of the art and the information that you are given about it. Ask dealers and collectors about buys they have made under the influence, and those who are willing to talk will tell you some real horror stories. Few have more than one incident to relate, however, because once they buy in a condition other than sober and realize what they've done the next day, they never buy that way again. Say no to drugs and alcohol and yes to buying art smart.

Don't Buy Art At Night. At night you tend to be less focused on rational, practical issues and more interested in entertaining yourself and having a good time. The chances of your buying art impulsively are greater at night than they are during the day. If you see an art piece you like while browsing through a gallery after normal business hours, put a hold on it and return the next day to look at it again and research it properly.

Don't Buy Art While You're On Vacation Unless You Investigate It as Thoroughly as You Do the Art You Buy While You're At Home. People on vacation are more carefree and unconcerned about how they spend their money than they are when they're at home. They tend to relax the rules a bit. This is one reason why you see so many art galleries in tourist areas. And guess what? A number of them are open at night!

Another mistake art buyers make on trips away from home is that they buy art not necessarily because it's good, but rather to remind them of what a wonderful time they had while they were away. Once again, remember that when you buy art, all you get is the art. You have to live with it long after the memories of that fantastic vacation fade.

Don't Buy Art Simply Because You're Charmed, Delighted, and Entertained By the Seller. When you buy art, you do not buy the personality of the gallery owner, the artist, or anyone else. Long after the seller is gone or that great time the two of you had together is forgotten, the art must continue to stand on its own as a quality example that's worth what you paid for it. If you're having trouble figuring out whether it's the art or the seller that is fascinating you more, take the art home on approval for a few days and study it in peace.

Don't Buy Art From Sellers Passing Through Town, At Special Close-Out Sales, At One-Shot Auctions, or Through Any Other Unestablished or Transient Outlets. No matter how attractive or reasonably priced the art for sale at these places or events may sound, confine your buying to respected dealers who have been in business for years and are known throughout the art community. Established dealers may not sell year-end close-out, get-it-while-you-can bargain art, but they do offer stability that transient sellers lack. Quality art does not change hands like leftover blouses on a close-out rack.

Don't Buy Art Because It Sounds Like a Great Bargain That's Almost Too Good to Be True. First of all, such art usually *is* too good to be true. Second, the fact that a work of art is presented to you as a "super deal" is not adequate justification for adding it to your collection. Look closer, and chances are it's not such a great deal after all. Sellers who offer incredible bargains usually provide somewhat suspect explanations about why their prices are so cheap. Watch out whenever you hear excuses like, "I need immediate cash to finance a new art buy," or "I have major expenses coming up and have to raise money," or "I could sell this for a lot more if only I had the time."

Don't Buy Art Over the Phone. This sounds unbelievable, but it actually happens. In spite of the fact that art is a visual and not an auditory commodity, dealers telemarket it and people buy it. The whole idea of buying an art piece based on the way a seller makes it sound during a telephone conversation is absurd to begin with. What's more, you have no idea who these sellers are, how reputable they are, what their galleries look like (assuming they even exist), how you would get your money back if you were not completely satisfied (even when they promise full immediate refunds), and so on.

Don't Buy Art By Name Only. You buy art because you like it, not because you hear that the artist is hot, that she's popular among investment bankers, that she's about to be featured in a national magazine, and so on. The first thing you look at is the art. The last thing you look at is the name of the artist.

Don't Buy Art Based Solely On the Fact That It's In a Beautiful Frame, On an Expensive Pedestal, and So On. Puttting bad art in great frames or on expensive pedestals, or presenting it in other lavish manners, is a trick some sellers use to fool unsuspecting buyers. Evaluate the art separately from the presentation.

Don't Buy Art Because You are Impressed By the Beauty Of the Gallery Selling It. The furnishings, decoration, and interior design of a gallery have no relation to the quality of the art that is being sold there. Some of the best art dealers operate out of the most modest surroundings, and some of the most unscrupulous dealers have beautifully appointed galleries.

Don't Buy Art When Sellers Change the Price Dramatically With Little Or No Provocation. Some galleries sell art by radically dropping prices right before your eyes. They appeal to the greed instinct. This procedure is designed to make you think you are getting a great bargain when in actuality you are usually getting schlock at heavily inflated prices.

For example, suppose a painting starts out at $10,000 and within thirty minutes the price has dropped to $6,500 because, according to the seller, you qualify for various special privileges. You mention that you're a collector, so the seller gives you a collector's discount; you mention that your aunt once worked in a frame shop, so he gives you a dealer discount; you tell him you work with computers, so he gives you the special high-tech businessperson's discount; and so on. The focus is off the art and on the plummeting price. Dealers who sell quality art rarely slash prices in this manner.

Don't Buy Art For Monetary Reasons Alone. Serious collectors buy art because they love art, not because they think they will be able to cash it in for profit at some later date. True, some art increases in value over time, but this is never adequate justification for deciding to buy or collect fine art. Remember: *Art increases in value a lot less often than most people think.*

Don't Buy Art Under Pressure. You should not select art for your collection based on the presence of a salesperson standing over your shoulder bombarding you with reasons why you should own it. When you begin to feel such pressure, leave the gallery.

Don't Buy Any Particular Art Or Artist Because All Your Friends Happen to Own One. Everyone has individual tastes and preferences in art. You buy what you like, and your friends buy what they like. When you buy what other people collect or tell you to buy, you deny yourself the thrill and pleasure of exploring, discovering, and expressing your own personal tastes.

Don't Buy Art That You See For Sale In Restaurants, Hotels, Department Stores, Or Any Other Nongallery Environments. Confine your buying to full-time art dealers whose only business is buying and selling art. Just as you do not rely on art dealers for overnight accomodations, meals, or clothing and appliances, you should not rely on hotels, restaurants, and department stores for art.

Don't Buy Art Based On Predictions. Beware when sellers begin talking about what's supposed to happen with art or artists at some point in the future. Base your art purchases on past performance, not on conjecture about what may or may not happen in the future. Predictions about how famous an artist will become or how much the art will appreciate in value are almost always designed as appeals to the greed instinct, nothing more.

Don't Buy Art Based Only On Emotional Response. The initial emotional response that you have to any art piece is no more than a very rough indication of how much or how little you like it. Temper the emotion with reason, and spend some serious time evaluating your reactions to any work of art before you buy.

Don't Buy Art Unless You're Absolutely Sure You Want to Own It. As long as you have even the slightest doubts, do not buy. You want the love affair you have with your art to last. You don't want that art to end up in your attic several months after you buy it.

Example 1: I know of a case in which an art dealer and an artist, both fascinating personalities, combined forces and sold plenty of art. They received a great deal of media attention and appeared at all the right social events. They were extremely popular and in demand. People loved to be around them and showed their appreciation by buying the artist's art. Together, this dealer and artist sold dozens of paintings at prices reaching into the tens of thousands of dollars each.

With the passage of time, the artist retired, the art dealer closed up his gallery, and both faded from the public eye. The market for the paintings, which were never that good in the first place, faded right along with the dealer and the artist. Collectors who paid huge prices for their art twenty and thirty years ago are now lucky if they can even get several hundred dollars each for them.

Make sure the art is at least as good as the personalities representing it. When it's not, as soon as the personalities are no longer available to stand by it while it is being sold, the market collapses. When you buy art, all you get is art.

Example 2: I know an art dealer who tells the story of how he once bought art under the influence of a few drinks—once and only once. This happened while he was attending an opening-night benefit at a large antique show. While there, he saw a painting in one dealer's booth that he thought looked great. It was a reasonably priced mountain scene painted in the 1920s. At that moment, he believed he could tell from looking at it that it was good enough to sell at his gallery. He was sure he'd heard of the artist before and felt no need to check any reference books before buying.

Here is what this dealer discovered the next day:

The artist had no track record. He was not listed in any reference books. The dealer had apparently confused the name with that of a different, more collectible artist. Furthermore, when he saw this painting in a sober state of mind, he realized it was terrible. He was astonished that he thought it had looked so wonderful in the antique dealer's booth just a few short hours before.

Example 3: The phenomenon of "the art opening" deserves special mention because you can be misled by what goes on at these events in so many different ways. If you become at all involved with art, sooner or later you will be invited to art openings.

In order to prepare yourself, let's attend an imaginary one now. Imagine yourself at an art opening at a beautifully appointed gallery. You sip champagne, nibble jumbo shrimp, rub shoulders with beautiful people, meet the artist, and view the art. You are in the eye of the storm, the center of the universe for this artist and his art. Everything about this environment is designed with three purposes in mind: sell, sell, and sell. Nowhere in the world does this artist's art look more appealing than it does in this gallery at this moment. And you are there.

You notice a stack of beautifully produced full-color exhibit catalogues on the counter. You pick one up and begin reading:

> Milton Mindholm's art transforms fact into fiction into fantasy and back into reality. He captures the highest essences of craftsmanship with techniques that at moments vibrate between brilliance and genius. He is unsurpassed in his ability to communicate direct mental images from his mind through his fingertips and outward onto blank canvas, at which point they evolve into unmistakable being.

You are impressed.

Mindholm's paintings are priced between $5,000 and $25,000. You are impressed again. Several pieces have little red dots next to them. You ask a staff person what the dots mean, and she tells you that they indicate works that have been sold. "People are buying," you think to yourself.

This looks to you like an exhibition of serious art by a serious artist, and some pieces are apparently being purchased for substantial amounts of money by serious collectors. From what you can see, money spent on Mindholm's art could well be money intelligently spent.

Now the facts:

- The size of the shrimp and the brand of champagne served at the opening have no relation to the quality of art that is being exhibited.

- The beauty, wealth, and fame of the people attending the opening have no relation to the quality of the art.

- The language used in the exhibition catalogue is only an indication of how good the writer is, not how good the artist is.

- The asking prices have no relation to the quality of the art.

- Little red dots are supposed to mean that art has been sold; however, that's not always the case. Some dealers place red dots on unsold art in order to make people believe it is selling.

A LOOK AHEAD

You now have all the basic tools necessary to successfully navigate your way around the art business, protect yourself from those who would take advantage, comparison shop, and, in the end, select those works of art you find the most appealing. As far as actually buying that art, however, you're only halfway there. You don't really know anything about the art you are considering other than what the sellers have told you about it—and that you like it. Acquiring additional information—learning the methods of art research— is the next major step in the buy art smart process and is the topic of the next chapter.

Part III: Research

Research is the cornerstone of intelligent art collecting. So far, you have made some specific art selections based primarily on how much you like the pieces. If you buy without researching them, however, you have no idea what you're buying, and you have no idea what you're getting for your money. Sure, sellers tell you plenty about your selections, but research corroborates these facts and reveals others that perhaps the sellers have overlooked or, in worst-case scenarios, deliberately not mentioned. Art research supplies you with facts you need to know before you buy.

Why is research necessary? Because facts affect value.

Not only do you do yourself a huge favor by researching potential purchases and getting the facts first, but you also do the entire art world a favor. The more people who research their art and buy intelligently, the more difficult a time galleries that sell inferior art and thrive on customers who buy impulsively have staying in business. Informed shoppers breed fair dealers who sell quality art at reasonable prices.

"But research sounds like such a complicated process," you say. You feel intimidated at the prospect of having to research art. You have no idea how to start, where to go, or what to do once you get there. "Research is only for art scholars, and you need a Ph.D. to do it, right?"

Wrong.

Anyone can learn to research works of art. Not only that, it's easy. You don't have to spend years training under museum curators and art historians. All the basic techniques you need to know are explained right here in Part III.

And not only is research easy to learn, but it's also quick to do. Once you know what you're doing, you can usually locate much of the information you need about a particular artist or work of art in less than an hour. Sure, more detailed research is necessary on occasion, but more often than not, a few minutes is all it takes.

Research is also rewarding. The more you know about art, the more you're able to appreciate it and the more enjoyable collecting becomes. The simple truth is that you experience art more fully and completely when you understand the facts and the history behind what you are looking at.

One more thing: By mastering the techniques of art research, you establish your independence as a collector. You eventually acquire the ability to analyze and evaluate every work of art you add to your collection entirely on your own, without the help of dealers or other authorities. You make your own decisions, and you do what's right for you. Based on your own judgments and inclinations, you buy art smart.

CHAPTER 10
Researching an Artist

Behind any work of art is an artist, a human being. The product of that artist's career is art, and because of facts peculiar to her and her alone, the art she creates is unique in ways that distinguish it from all other art. By understanding the progression of events in that artist's life and career, you are better able to understand her art. Add these facts to your visual appreciation of the art itself, and you achieve a much deeper sense of what that art is all about.

On the practical side, facts about any artist, her career, and what she has accomplished relate directly to the dollar value of her art, its collectibility, and its salability in the marketplace. With adequate information, you can decide whether or not an art piece is worth adding to your collection and whether or not you are spending your money wisely by buying it.

The great majority of information you need to obtain and evaluate is as basic as where an artist was born, where she studied art, how old she is, how long she has been an artist, what exhibitions she has participated in, and so on. You can learn plenty about an artist and her art from simple biographical data like that.

This procedure is similar to verifying the qualifications of any professionals you are interested in hiring before they perform services for you; you want to make sure you are getting quality services (or products) from individuals who know what they're doing. Just as you hire a lawyer to handle your legal affairs and hire an accountant to keep your books, when you buy an art piece, you do, in a sense, hire the artist who created that piece. You pay that artist for services (products) rendered. And if you're like most people, you want your art to be created by qualified artists who charge fees commensurate with the products—the art—they provide.

Buying art based on an artist's credentials is not necessarily a foolproof method of determining whether or not you are spending your money wisely, but in the great majority of cases, the more distinguished the artist's career, the safer you are buying that artist's art. Furthermore, accomplishments in art stand for all time and continue to affect marketability long after the artist has passed on. Below is an example of how even a small amount of biographical data can aid you in a decision-making process.

Suppose you have selected two very similar paintings for possible purchase, both the same size, subject matter, quality, and style. You like them both equally well and have decided to choose one to buy. Each is priced at

$2,000. One is by an artist named John Doeman, the other by Henrietta Homer. You find out that Homer was born in 1920, began painting seriously in 1938, and has been an artist full time since 1948. Doeman, who was also born in 1920, recently took up painting and is having the first show of his work at the gallery where you saw it. What can you either assume or conclude from these facts? Plenty!

Conclusions about Henrietta Homer: She makes her living as an artist. She has been painting for decades and is established in her career. She has proven herself as an artist and survived financially for over forty years by selling her art. Most likely, she is going to continue painting and not give up art for another career. If she has sold successfully for so many years, she has certainly produced a substantial body of work, most of which is probably pretty good.

Conclusions about John Doeman: He is an unproven commodity. He started painting only recently and even though the quality of the painting you like is comparable to that of Homer's, you have no way to tell, due to Doeman's relative inexperience, whether he will be able to maintain that quality level in all his work and eventually be considered equal in stature and accomplishment to Homer. In addition, you have no idea whether his art is consistently good and salable or whether he just happened to get lucky on this one particular painting. You have no idea how many paintings Doeman has sold during his short career—certainly fewer than Homer. You have no way of knowing whether he will produce a sufficient body of work to become recognized as an artist, or whether he will stop painting next month and fade into permanent obscurity.

You rarely have so little information to go on as you do in this example, but you see how far you can get on a minimum number of facts. Assuming you are concerned about how you spend your $2,000 and don't want to take any unnecessary risks (which is exactly the way beginners should approach art collecting), you should buy the Homer, not the Doeman. You get a work of art by a long-established and accepted artist if you go with Homer. With Doeman, you're not quite sure what you get.

How would you decide between these two paintings knowing nothing about either Homer or Doeman? You could flip a coin. You could put them side by side and stare at them hoping one might start looking slightly better than the other. No matter what you do, though, you'd be buying blind.

"But," you argue, "if I decide I like the Doeman, shouldn't I buy it regardless of what the facts are?" Absolutely. You're perfectly entitled to buy it, no matter how many facts you have and no matter what those facts are.

What's important is that you have those facts and know what you are buying before you buy it, and also that you have no misconceptions about Homer or Doeman and their careers. Informed buyers make smart collectors.

HOW TO LOCATE BIOGRAPHICAL DATA

The primary source of artist data is printed information found in books, encyclopedias, directories, exhibition catalogues, price references, newspaper or magazine articles, and so on. All major public or university library art departments, art museums, and better art galleries have substantial collections of these reference materials on hand. The references we are talking about here, the ones you will learn how to use, are standard and accepted by all in the art community.

For those of you who prefer to buy your own art reference books and would rather not use libraries, Appendix 6 contains a list of specialized art-reference booksellers. Art museum bookstores are also a good source of reference books, but their art books tend to be a little more general in nature than those sold by the booksellers listed in Appendix 6. Specialized art booksellers are good to know about, because if you decide to get at all involved in collecting, having certain basic references within easy reach is essential.

The types of references you will be using are briefly summarized by category here. Many of the more important basic references in each category are listed in Appendix 2 with brief comments about each following the listings. This appendix by no means covers all art reference books, but it is reasonably comprehensive and includes more than enough basic resources to get you started no matter what artist you are researching.

By the way, don't be intimidated by the total number of reference books listed in Appendix 2. Once you know how to research, you develop a feel for which references in particular will be the most helpful to you on a case-by-case basis. You will rarely have to check dozens of titles, but rather just the few that relate to your specific collecting situation.

Artist Indexes (See Appendix 2). Artist indexes are a good place to begin any research. These references contain names of hundreds of thousands of artists of all time periods and nationalities. They are alphabetized lists of names, usually accompanied by basic biographical information such as birth and death dates, nationalities, and specialties (painter, sculptor, etcher, etc.).

Indexes are important because, along with basic data, they list titles of additional art reference books that include more detailed information about the artist you are researching. You then locate these references and use them to assemble complete biographical profiles. Be aware that art indexes do not always list every additional reference that contains information, so continue researching even after checking the books that indexes refer you to.

Each index lists artists slightly differently, but an average entry looks something like this:

Quinara, Samaras; 1890–1969, Brazilian Painter, EncArtAmer.

From this entry you can see that Samaras Quinara lived from 1890 to 1969, that he was a Brazilian painter, and that further information about him can be located in a reference that is abbreviated as "EncArt Amer." Full bibliographical information (title, author, publisher, copyright data, etc.) about abbreviated resources can be located at the beginnings of all indexes. In this case, EncArtAmer refers to an artist reference called *Enciclopedia del Arte en America,* which focuses on North, Central, and South American artists.

Artist Encyclopedias (See Appendix 2). These multivolume sets supply information about artists of all time periods and all nationalities. The three most frequently used encyclopedias, *Benezit, Theime-Becker,* and *Theime-Becker's* supplement (called *Vollmer*), are written in French and German, respectively, so you may need to have entries translated when you locate them. All three contain information about artists from around the world, although they are best for researching European artists. Other more specialized encyclopedias, some of which are listed in the appendix, include only artists from specific parts of the world. This is not a complete list, so check with art dealers, art librarians, or other experts for the names of additional specialized encyclopedias as you need them.

Artist Dictionaries (See Appendix 2). These references, which are usually in one or two volumes, are more specific than general encyclopedias. They might include artists from only one country, one discipline, one time period, one state, one sex, and so on. For example, you can find dictionaries specific to categories such as the following: artists of a particular state, American Indian artists, nineteenth-century English artists, women artists, marine artists, naive artists, and so on. Some of the major artist dictionaries are listed in Appendix 2, but once again, this is by no means an exhaustive list. As with encyclopedias, learn which dictionaries are most applicable to your specific needs.

Artist Annuals and Directories (See Appendix 2). These references are published regularly and are constantly being revised, updated, and enlarged. Some are published annually, while others are published every few years. Like dictionaries, artist annuals and directories list artists alphabetically and usually according to specific criteria, such as the type of art they produce, the state or country they live in, and so on. *Who's Who in American Art,* for instance, is published every other year and includes only Americans. Once again, the titles listed in the appendix do not form an exhaustive list of these kinds of references.

Art Archives and Files. Art archives and files are collections of documents, news clippings, correspondences, catalogues, writings, and other miscellaneous information about art and artists. Archives and files often include data that is unpublished and is not available anywhere else. The major American art archives, called the Archives of American Art, is headquartered at the Smithsonian Institute in Washington, D.C. (the phone number is 202-357-2781). Many major national (and local) libraries, museums, historical societies, art associations, and art institutes maintain files and archives, as do some dealers. Consult experts and check specific institutions according to whom you are researching to see whether relevant archives exist and, if so, where they are located.

Auction Records and Price Guides (See Appendix 2). These references will be discussed at length in Part IV. Briefly, price references tell you whether works by particular artists have sold at public sales (primarily auctions) and either specifically or approximately how much those works have sold for.

When you first start researching artists, have art librarians, art dealers, and other professionals walk you through the basics, step by step. This is the best way to learn what you're doing, to identify the specific references best suited to your needs, and, eventually, to learn how to streamline the process. Experts can teach you how to use any reference book within a matter of minutes. Artist research is really that easy!

Even on you're own, learning how to use books to research artists is not difficult. All you do is check those references listed in Appendix 2 that appear to be relevant to your situation one by one, preferably in the order they have been summarized here (indexes first, encyclopedias next, and so on). This way, you maximize your chances of locating the information you need. The next few paragraphs cover several additional research pointers.

Whenever You Research, Check as Many Relevant References as Possible. This is especially true when you're starting out. Since you do not know which books to go to immediately and what their respective strengths and weaknesses are, you have to look in every one that could possibly help you. This exercise also gives you practice researching and familiarizes you with what specific references are all about.

If You Find an Artist Listed In One Book, Don't Stop Looking and Assume You Have All the Information You Need. Different books often contain different information about the same artist, and combining what you find yields the best results. If you don't find an artist listed in the first two or three books you check, do not give up and decide that the artist is a total unknown. Continue checking; then decide.

Approach the Task of Gathering Information as though You Were Writing an Essay Entitled "The Life of an Artist." Write down or photocopy every listing or entry you find. Do this whether or not you think that what you read has any significance or relation to the artist's art. The truth is that *everything* you find is relevant.

Here's an extreme example of information that may seem irrelevant at first, but actually isn't. Suppose you have selected a work of art for possible purchase and discover that the artist murdered one of his models in 1942. Do you want to own a work by this artist? Maybe you do, but chances are you want to own it less than you did before finding out that information. A number of collectors would refuse to collect this artist if they became aware of the murder, and that effect, in turn, decreases the artist's value and desirability in the marketplace. The 1942 murder has no direct bearing on the quality of the art, but it certainly affects the artist's collectibility.

You won't have to go much further than the Appendix 2 references with the great majority of artists you research. The reason is that most artists are not that widely written about and are listed nowhere other than in the standard references, archives, and files. The more well-known artists are, however, the more they have been written about, the more information exists, and the more you need it in order to make informed decisions.

Information about better-known artists can be located in numerous books, exhibition catalogues, and other publications in addition to those references listed in Appendix 2. The most famous artists are included in dozens of references; some even have entire books written about them (books about single artists are known as *monographs*). If you intend to collect art by important artists, have experts teach you how to research and assemble data from multiple sources. Such advanced research techniques are beyond the scope of this book.

HOW TO INTERPRET THE RESULTS OF ARTIST RESEARCH

Finding an artist listed in standard references is a good sign, but that fact alone does not bestow instant collectibility or justify the price that is being asked for the art. You must know how to interpret those listings in order to get an accurate idea of how accomplished the artist really is. Some of the general ways that information you find in books affects an artist's market are discussed here. Be aware that none of these is an absolute and that no single one being true is enough to base your final conclusions on.

The More Books That Include an Artist, the More Collectible His or Her Art Is. An artist you find listed in twenty books is better known than one listed in only two books.

The More Significant the References That Include an Artist Are, the More Significant the Artist Is. For example, an artist listed only in a dictionary of Ohio artists and nowhere else is less important than one listed in all major art encyclopedias of the world.

The More Mentions an Artist Has In Any Given Reference and the Longer Those Mentions Are, the More Collectible His or Her Art Is. A detailed two-page listing is more significant than a brief two-line entry.

The Longer an Artist Has Been Included In Books, the More Collectible His or Her Art Is. For example, a contemporary artist who has been included in basic references ever since she started painting in the 1930s is more well-known and well-recognized than an artist of the same age who has been included only since 1985.

The More Detailed the Listings Are in Terms Of Art-Related Accomplishments, the More Collectible the Artist Is. An artist who has participated in numerous national shows and exhibits, won awards in prestigious competitions, exhibited around the world, placed work in museums, and been represented by widely respected galleries is more important that one who has been involved in only small local or regional events, been represented only by one local gallery, and so on.

The More Respected the Authors Are and the More Widely Accepted the References, the More Seriously You May Consider the Artists They Write About. For example, museum curators, art scholars, and art historians who write legitimate scholarly texts are involved in the most unbiased sorts of writing. On the other hand, dealers who write and publish their own catalogues about artists they represent or promote have personal interest and financial gain in mind. As a result, they are naturally prejudiced in favor of those artists and don't always present the facts accurately. Check with experts whenever you have questions about whether a reference is legitimate and accepted as standard by the art community or is a vanity publication designed to make money for an art dealer.

The More Respected the Institution Publishing the Book is, the More Seriously You May Consider the Information You Locate. For example, a listing in a major museum exhibition catalogue, university press book, or standard artist encyclopedia is more significant than a listing in a catalogue published by a small regional or local art association.

With Respect to Price Records, Artists Who Sell Works for More Money Are Generally More Important and Collectible Than Those Who Sell for Less. That's not much to go on concerning price, but it's enough for now. You'll read plenty more about art prices and how to evaluate them in Part IV.

ASSESSING THE FACTS

Once you have a general idea of what books list an artist, who wrote them, and how frequently and extensively that artist is listed, you have to focus on the individual facts you find. These facts fall into specific categories and mean certain things. Below are described the categories of facts you normally encounter, a brief summary of what they mean, how to interpret them, and how they tend to affect an artist's market.

Birth and Death Dates. An artist's age is a good thing to know. From it you can determine how long he has been an artist, how old he was when he started, how old he is now, and so on. For example, if you like to buy conservatively, as you should in the early stages of your collecting, buying established artists who have been active for decades is less risky than buying art by young artists who are just starting out.

Where and With Whom an Artist Studied. These facts are interesting to know, but they have little bearing on an artist's collectibility or reputation. Studying under famous artists or graduating from the finest art schools is a step in the right direction, but what really counts is what the artist accomplishes after completing that education. Self-taught artists with little or no formal schooling can be just as accomplished as those with years of training. Watch out for dealers who try to sell you on artists just because those artists had great teachers or graduated from the best schools.

Organizational Memberships. The organizations an artist belongs to are not necessarily an indication of how collectible that artist is. Many groups or associations allow anyone to join. Certain memberships, however, do indicate a level of accomplishment on the artist's part, especially organizations that only admit new members by vote. For example, being elected as a National Academician is a high honor and a major accomplishment for any American artist. Whatever art you collect, find out the names of the most important and prestigious organizations that the artists who produce that type of art can belong to.

Where an Artist Has Exhibited. The more recognized the institutions where an artist has exhibited, the better. For example, showing a painting at the Metropolitan Museum of Art is a more prestigious accomplishment than showing one at the Tinytown Zucchini Bazaar.

Group Exhibitions Versus One-Person Exhibitions. As an accomplishment, having a one-person show is superior to appearing in a group show. For example, having a one-person show at the Metropolitan Museum of Art is a far greater accomplishment than showing one work of art at that museum in a group show with 300 other artists.

Awards Received. Awards always speak well for an artist, but you have to differentiate between important awards and not-so-important ones. Winning a gold medal at a major international art exhibition is obviously more significant than winning the Minnie Ginchflower Award for Sunday Painting at the Hooper Valley Bake Sale.

Public or Corporate Collections Owning Works By an Artist. The fact that museums or corporations own works by an artist is an indication that the art has been recognized as significant by certain experts and authorities within the art community. You have to be a little careful here because although most collection listings are legitimate, some artists claim to be in certain collections when, in fact, they are not. If you have any questions about collection listings, contact the specific institutions and ask whether work by the artist is actually in their *permanent* collections. One additional point: Make sure that listed corporations are known and recognized for the quality of their art collections.

Private Collections Owning Works By an Artist. This is a sticky area. Basically, major private collections known for having quality art are good for an artist to be in and good for you to know about. Other collections, even though they sound impressive, may be nothing. For example, suppose you read that an artist has an etching in the collection of Countess Estrelita of Tyrolia. This sounds significant, but for all you know the Countess may have no taste in art, the artist may have given her the etching free, or her entire "collection" may consist only of that one etching.

Auction and Other Price Records. Briefly, finding any price results whatsoever on an artist is good, and the higher they are, the better. Interpreting price records will be discussed at length in Part IV.

When you're just starting out, always double-check your final evaluations with experts. Get a consensus from those "in the know." Make sure you are reading and interpreting the data correctly and are not jumping to any erroneous conclusions.

WHAT TO DO WHEN YOU COME UP EMPTY-HANDED

Suppose that, after all your research, you come up empty-handed? You find absolutely no data on the artist you are researching, and all you have to go on is what the seller has told you. This is never good, and whenever you find yourself in a dataless situation, you've got a problem—and several possible solutions.

The most common reason why people come up empty-handed is that either they shortcut their research by not checking enough references or they research only at small local libraries or other institutions with inadequate art reference sections. The solution: Try at least two more large libraries in major cities and check more references. Also, explain your situation to expert librarians or curators and ask them for advice, in case you've overlooked something.

If you still find no information, it could be that you are researching a very minor artist who is not accomplished enough to be listed in references. This doesn't necessarily mean you should forget about buying the art. You can, of course, buy whatever you want, no matter how little-known the artist is. What a lack of artist data *does* mean, though, is that you probably shouldn't be paying too much for that artist's work.

You have three possible options in any circumstance where research yields nothing:

- If the art is inexpensive and you like it, go ahead and buy it. You're not risking anything.

- If the piece of art is expensive, if you enjoy taking risks, and if you don't care how you spend your money, go ahead and buy it. (This is not a particularly popular option.)

- Forget about buying the art, no matter what the price, but especially if it's expensive. Look for another artist whose work you like just as much and who has a documented and researchable track record.

Example 1: Imagine you are considering buying a painting by John James Burton and find this listing in a standard art reference book:

> Burton, John James
> Painter
> Born: Roundtree, Virginia; May 22, 1945. Studied: University of Texas, BA; Oregon Art Institute, MFA. Works Held: Smithville Art Museum, Municipal Museum, International Farm Equipment Company collection. Exhibited: Modern Art Museum, St. Louis, 1975; National Art Association, Wash. D.C., 1978; Municipal Museum (one-man), San Francisco, 1982; Boston Art Museum Spring Show, 1988. Awards: Second Prize, Boston Art Museum, 1988. Member: American Art Association. Mailing address: 2345 Union St., Wildflower, AZ 11111.

You can tell from reading this listing that Burton is a relatively young artist who has achieved some recognition. So far, he has an impressive track record. He has exhibited nationally and has work in several collections. He has had a one-man museum show and won an award. Assuming you want to know more, here's how you can follow up on this data:

- Contact the two museums and one business that own his art. Find out the circumstances of the purchases or donations, whether the art hangs on a permanent basis, whether they can supply you with additional biographical information, and so on.

- Contact the Municipal Museum for further information on Burton and details on the one-man show. Maybe they'll be able to send you a catalogue of that show.

- Find out how important the Boston Art Museum Spring Show is and how important the award is that Burton received at that show.

- Find out how important the American Art Association is and what its membership requirements are.

- Contact Burton himself and see whether he can supply you with a complete résumé of his career.

Example 2: Not all art galleries rely on standard reference listings and traditional measures of artistic accomplishment to sell their artists to the public. Some try to distract you from the facts. I can think of several galleries that use well-known public figures to promote artists in much the same way that advertising agencies use athletes or entertainers to endorse athletic shoes, automobiles, candy bars, and other consumer products. Rather than offer legitimate data about their artists, these galleries show you pictures of these artists in the company of well-known personalities, give you the names of famous people (again of the non-art-expert variety) who own the art, or use other celebrity-related tactics to convince you to buy.

Know that celebrity endorsements mean nothing unless those celebrities also happen to be art experts. No matter how glamorous or important a gallery makes an artist look, standard art references give you the straight story on fame and accomplishment.

Example 3: Researching and finding out nothing about an artist can be just as telling as finding pages of information. I have visited a number of galleries that exhibit works by artists whom the gallery owners claim are nationally known or even world famous—and who also happen to be artists I have never heard of. The art is frequently accompanied by impressive-looking certificates or brochures that make claims about how famous the artists are. I sometimes research these artists out of curiosity, mainly because I'm surprised I've never heard of them and suspect that they're not as well-known as the galleries say they are.

Some turn out to be listed in no standard reference books or other publications where "famous" artists are normally written about. Others are virtually unknown outside the galleries that sell their art. The truth is that some artists are misrepresented by their dealers as being far more important than they actually are. Always corroborate dealer claims with your own independent research.

Example 4: Some "art references," especially those published by special interests, have a tendency to bend the truth or misstate facts. I recall an occasion on which I met with an artist who gave me her promotional brochure. She had written it herself, paid for it herself, and designed it to promote her art and her art only. On top of that, she was great at promoting herself in person. She regularly sold her sculptures at what I considered to be impressively high prices.

Her brochure contained color illustrations of her art, laudatory information about her career, and names of private and public collectors who owned her work. It also listed several museums as owning sculptures. I did not bother to check whether any of these claims were true because I did not plan on doing any business with this artist. I filed the brochure away and forgot about it.

Several months later, while speaking with another dealer, this artist's name came up. I told him about her brochure and mentioned that her work was apparently in several important museum collections. He laughed, told me that no museums owned her work, and went on to explain what the truth really was.

According to him, she had mailed sculptures free of charge to these museums as donations. The museums had accepted them, but not for their collections. They were probably sold at white elephant sales or other fund-raising events, the proceeds of which were used to finance museum operations. Works by this artist were not recorded in official museum records as being in any of their permanent collections.

Example 5: Sometimes gallery owners are the ones who neglect to research artists, and other dealers or collectors are the ones who profit. I once made a great bargain buy at a high-profile gallery that normally sells art at top retail prices. The owner had hung and priced a small painting by an important midwestern artist, apparently without researching it. I recognized it to be worth about $5,000. It was priced at just under $1,000, and I bought it on the spot.

While I was paying for the picture, I asked this dealer what he knew about the artist. He said he had found small bits of information here and there, but nothing substantial. I asked him what reference books he had checked and he told me. He had researched only briefly, and the books he had used were not the best references for that artist. If he had checked more in depth, he would have discovered that an entire book had been written about this artist and that several other books contained entire chapters on the painter's illustrious career.

A LOOK AHEAD

Assembling biographical data about an artist is your first step in research. Assuming the artist remains under consideration after you evaluate your findings, you must now turn your attention to the particular work of art that you have selected. Researching and evaluating that single piece of art is essential in determining whether or not it's right for your collection. The next chapter explains the procedures for researching a specific work.

CHAPTER 11

Researching a Work of Art

Imagine two different works of art by the same artist. One is priced at $500, and the other weighs in at a hefty $50,000. This may sound absurd—that the same artist could have produced both—but it's a relatively common occurrence. The difference in price between an artist's cheapest and most expensive art is often quite large.

How can this be? The answer is simple. The same artist can produce great art, good art, average art, terrible art, big art, little art, one-of-a-kind art, mass-edition art, and so on. The range and variety of art that the average artist produces during his or her lifetime can be astonishing.

Unfortunately, you cannot easily tell what works by an artist deserve to sell for a lot of money and what works should be selling for just a little. No standard grading or rating system exists for labeling significance, excellence, quality, or inferiority of all this art. You cannot instantly tell by seeing a rating label or stamp on a work of art whether it is Class A, Four Star, Extra Fine, Grade A, a second, or an irregular, but you can make these distinctions if you know how. *Methods exist for determining the relative importance of any art piece in terms of the total output of the artist who created it.*

Many novice art collectors never even think about relative importance or significance. They make the mistake of viewing an art piece as an isolated quantity and neglect to relate it to anything else the artist has ever produced. As long as it's by the artist, they reason, that's good enough for them. A Picasso is a Picasso is a Picasso. In dealer jargon, they buy the name and not the art. A common result of this oversight is that these collectors end up overpaying for inferior art.

For example, I know a collector who was interested in buying a painting by a collectible American artist. He had seen the artist's work at several galleries, liked it, and was aware that it usually sold in the $3,000-to-$5,000 range. He decided to shop around until he found just the right picture.

One day at a gallery, he saw a painting by this artist for only $900. It looked similar to some of the more expensive ones he'd seen at other galleries, and it was about the same size. He decided he'd discovered a major bargain and bought it instantly. He now owned that painting he'd always wanted.

This story does not end happily ever after, however. The collector brought me the painting and proudly showed me what a great buy he'd made. I took one look at it and had to inform him that his treasure was indeed by the artist, but that was the only positive thing I could say about it. I told him that not only was it a poor example of the artist's work, but it was probably the worst example I'd ever seen. His "bargain" was overpriced even at $900 and was worth only $500 at best.

This collector made two common errors. First, he assumed that as long as the artist had painted it, it had to be good. Second, he believed that all paintings by the artist were worth about the same amount of money—$3,000 to $5,000 each. If he had known how to compare his $900 special to other paintings by the artist instead of only looking at name and price, chances are good that he never would have bought it.

The important point to remember is that when you purchase a work of art, you do not buy an isolated item; you buy a portion of an artist's total output, and you have to evaluate it in terms of that output. You want that portion, small as it is, to be a good example of the artist's work, not a poor one.

Let's assume you are in the process of researching one of your selections for possible purchase. You assemble biographical data according to the guidelines laid out in the previous chapter and decide that art by this artist is worth buying for your collection. Now you have to evaluate the art.

1. *Begin by reviewing the results of your biographical research and looking for clues about what the artist does best.* Note any statements relating specifically to the artist's art. Perhaps she won an award for an oil painting of a New York City street scene. Maybe you'll see a sentence describing her as a well-known animal sculptor. Note any information regarding what this artist creates that is most recognized by those in the art community.

2. *Familiarize yourself with the artist's total output.* Find out what she has produced so far in her career, when she did it, what it looks like, how her style has changed over the years, and so on. You have to know and understand the whole in order to properly evaluate the individual parts.

3. *Study as many examples of the artist's art as you can.* See them at galleries; in exhibits; in books, magazines, or catalogues; and wherever else you can locate them. Note characteristics of the most expensive examples you can find; note characteristics of the least expensive ones. See what the price differences are between the high-end art and the low-end art done by the artist.

4. *Ask dealers, collectors, and other experts familiar with the artist's work to tell you what the artist is best (and least) known for.* Have them describe the qualities of those works. Whenever possible, view and discuss actual examples in the company of these experts.

Combine the results of research, repeated viewings, and conversations with experts with your answers to the questions detailed below. Keep in mind when researching the relative importance of a work of art that you will occasionally find exceptions to these general rules and tendencies. They do, however, hold true in the great majority of cases.

Is the Art an Actual Work of Art Executed By the Artist Whose Signature It Bears, or Is It a Photographic Reproduction? Many art galleries sell pencil-signed (and sometimes numbered) photographic reproductions of works of art; some galleries sell them without even the pencil signatures. These prints are *not* created by the artists whose signatures they bear—they are produced by the photographers who photograph the actual works of art and the printing companies that print the results of those photo sessions. All the artists do is spend several seconds pencil-signing (and sometimes numbering) them.

Because photographic reproductions are *not* actual works of art, they are insignificant in terms of an artist's total output. In fact, it is debatable whether they should even be classified as part of an artist's total output. If you have any doubts about art you are looking at, ask one simple question: "Is this an actual work of art or a photographic reproduction?" Get the answer in writing.

Assuming your selection is an actual work of art created by the artist whose signature it bears, continue with the questions listed here.

Is the Art Major or Minor? The terms *major* and *minor* relate to the scope and complexity of individual works of art. A major work is often better composed, more original, more detailed, better executed, more complex, and larger in size than is a minor work. Important major pieces display an artist's total range of talents. A major work takes more time and effort to produce than a minor one, and, consequently, major works cost more than minor ones.

Many collectors make two common and often costly mistakes of oversimplifying the differences between major and minor, so before going any further, two warnings are in order. First, don't confuse major with "good" and minor with "bad." Minor works can be just as well-executed as major ones. They're simply not as broad in scope or as complex on certain levels.

Second, don't confuse major with "bigger" and minor with "smaller." Bigger is not necessarily better, more important, or worth more money. A well-known art professor of the 1940s and 1950s, the time when large abstract paintings were coming into fashion, used to put in his two cents on the size issue by telling his students, "If you can't paint good, paint big." Never judge works of art based on size alone.

Enough warnings—now for a pop quiz. Consider two paintings by an artist known for his farm scenes. Let's say they are equal in size and painted equally well. One shows a red barn and silo surrounded by a field of corn. The other shows a red barn and silo, but it also shows a house, three children playing on the front porch, two pickup trucks in the driveway, a chicken coop with chickens, several different fields of crops, another field being plowed by a farmer on a tractor, the next-door-neighbor's farmhouse and barn in the distance, and an approaching thunderstorm. Which one has the characteristics of a major piece?

Now imagine that the first painting measures 8 by 10 inches and the second measures 30 by 50 inches. Assuming again that they are painted equally well, which one is more worthy of being called major?

In both cases, if you answered the second, you're absolutely right. The second is far more detailed, and the composition is much more complex. In terms of labor alone, the artist would have to spend many more hours conceiving and executing the second than the first.

The best examples of any artist's work are referred to as "major," and no matter what artist you are interested in, you should tend toward major examples in your collecting, whenever possible, and avoid very minor ones. This does not mean that you zero in on the most monumental work an artist has ever produced, but it does mean that you at least look for art that has some characteristics of the artist's major pieces. If all you can afford is a minor work, a low-end piece, you may wish to move to a more affordable artist. Owning a minor example by a big-name artist is not necessarily better than owning major example by a less well-known artist.

You don't always have to buy major, though, or even close to it. If you love the art and it happens to be minor, at least make sure that it's competently executed and fairly priced. Then go ahead and buy it.

As an aside, you'll find minor works to be overpriced much more often than you'll find major works to be overpriced. Too many people—dealers and collectors alike—either promote or subscribe to the myth that the signature is more important than the art and that anything with the right name on it has to be expensive. The truth is that even the greatest artists produce minor, inferior, and just plain bad works of art that should be priced far below what their best efforts cost.

Is the Art Typical or Atypical of the Artist's Work? All artists are known for producing certain types of art. To begin with, most artists are best known for specializing in a particular medium. One may be a sculptor in bronze, the next a painter in oils, another a lithographer. Getting more specific, each artist is known for producing certain subject matters within their recognized mediums. The bronze sculptor may be known for his depictions of wild game animals, the painter for her abstracts in oils, and the lithographer for his Paris street scenes. These works of art would be considered "typical" of these artists.

If You're a Beginning Collector, Play It Conservative and Tend Toward Collecting Typical Works, That Is, the Art That Particular Artists Are Best Known for Producing. In the above three cases, these would be a bronze wild animal sculpture, an abstract oil painting, or a lithographed Paris street scene. In general, focus on typical works and avoid atypical, experimental, offbeat, or unusual works of art that artists do not have reputations for producing. Continuing our earlier example, avoid a floral still-life painting done by the animal sculptor, a landscape etching by the abstract painter, or a watercolor coastal scene by the lithographer. Even though the quality of these items may be good or their prices substantially less than those of the typical works (as is often the case), they do not ordinarily make good buys. At worst, you could get stuck with a one-of-a-kind experiment that an artist tried, failed at, and decided never to attempt again.

When knowledgeable dealers and collectors think of a particular artist, they tend to think of that artist in terms of what he or she is best known for producing. When they buy that artist, they buy in those terms also. Take the animal sculptor who works in bronze, for example. Because the art community identifies him as a bronze sculptor who depicts animals, that floral still-life painting he did will be considered an oddity and have little appeal for collectors of his work.

Atypical works are not always ignored, however. Experienced collectors, for example, sometimes recognize atypical works as being outstanding and worthwhile owning no matter who did them. Advanced collectors who are in the process of forming definitive collections of particular artists' works also buy atypical pieces from time to time.

A final note is in order here. Some artists work in more than one medium or are competent in more than one subject matter. In these cases, find out what they are the most proficient in, as well as what they don't do all that well. For example, an artist who paints, sculpts, and etches may be best known for her sculptures of famous people, reasonably well-respected for her paintings of New England hills, and not particularly well-thought-of for her etchings, no matter what their subjects are.

When Does the Art Date From? *Art from certain periods in artists' careers is often more collectible than the art from other periods.* Career high points can happen at any time—some early, some in the middle, some late. For instance, Paul Gauguin's Tahitian period is known to be his most brilliant creatively.

When researching an artist, determine these artistic peaks from biographical data and by speaking with experts. Get to know when the best periods are and what art from those periods looks like. Art from the best periods is often the most important, the most collectible, and commands the highest prices.

Artists also experience career low points—difficult times, times of change, times when whatever they produce just doesn't quite work. Work from less productive periods is worth substantially less than work from peak periods. Sometimes, for instance, you find art that at first seems relatively inexpensive, but once you start researching it, you discover that it's cheap because it has that "low-point look" that no collectors are interested in owning.

How Original Is the Art? *Original compositions, techniques, and subject matters in art are more significant and collectible than are repeats of things that have already been done.* Here we're talking about art that the art community recognizes as a step forward in an artist's career or, even better, works that advance the evolution of art as a whole. The example below helps to clarify what the term *original* means.

Suppose an artist devotes all his creative energies to producing twenty sculptures for a gallery show. They're like nothing he's ever done before. He agonizes over them for months, experimenting and trying hundreds of different compositional options before settling on just the right look.

The artist shows the sculptures at an art gallery, and they receive instant acclaim from prominent members of the art community. Collectors also love what they see, and the show sells out within three weeks. The artist decides that since this work sold so well, he's going to produce the same sculptures over again. This time, he makes forty pieces, and within several months they sell out once more. By now, the artist feels he has found a formula for producing art that he can sell regularly and decides to make nothing but these sculptures for the rest of his life.

When dealers, collectors, and other experts look back on this artist's career, they will regard the sculptures from that very first show and ones produced shortly after as being the most original—and thus the most significant, collectible, and valuable. Ones produced five or ten or twenty years later, even though they look the same as the earlier ones, will be less desirable because they are basically reenactments, repeats of creative moments that the artist experienced years before. They lack the originality of the earliest pieces.

The ultimate repeats are works of art produced by artists who do nothing original, but rather copy what other artists have already done. Continuing with the sculpture example, suppose another sculptor sees how successful the first sculptor is and decides to produce similar sculptures himself. He rides the first artist's coattails and attempts to cash in on the collecting frenzy. His sculptures completely lack originality, are purely decorative, and are nothing more than knock-offs.

With respect to price, the most original art should cost the most; repeats by the artist who first conceived those originals should cost less; and repeats by other artists who copy the original artist should cost the least. Watch out for galleries that price any types of repeats close to what originals are selling for. These galleries are attempting to victimize inexperienced collectors who don't know enough to tell the difference. When you're just starting out, rely on the advice of experts and consult biographical data whenever you have questions about the degree of originality.

How Well Done Is the Art? Determining quality in art is important. It's also difficult to do when you've been collecting only a short while. *The only way you learn to recognize quality is through experience—by looking at all the art you possibly can, learning about the artists, listening to the experts, and learning what makes any given piece good, better, or best.* A work of art may be typical, original, from the right period, and so on, but if the quality isn't there, it's not worth buying. When you're starting out, protect yourself on the quality issue by consulting experts and dealing with galleries that have experience selling the type of art you want.

Example 1: Early in my career, an art dealer offered me a darkish misty sunset scene by a well-known American artist. He wanted $2,000 for the painting and told me that it was a great bargain at that price. He backed up his claim by telling me that two paintings by this artist, approximately the same size as mine, had recently sold at auction for over $10,000 each. He intimated that I would have no trouble doubling or even tripling my money. I believed him and bought the picture.

Several days later, I discovered that the seller had misrepresented the painting by not giving me the full auction story and that, unfortunately, my "bargain" was worth nowhere near what I had paid for it. Yes, the impressive sales had taken place, but both high auction prices were for snow scenes, the scenes the artist was most famous for painting. My painting was atypical, nothing like what collectors wanted, difficult to sell, and worth only about $1,000 at the most.

If I had known more about typical versus atypical subject matters at that time, I could have saved myself hundreds of dollars as well as the headache of trying to resell that painting. I took time to learn how to make this distinction, however, immediately after I realized what a very poor buy I had made. I also decided never to do business with that dealer again.

Example 2: Suppose that you are thinking about buying a watercolor of the Rocky Mountains by an artist named Maria Mathews and you discover certain details about her career. Here are each of those details followed by an explanation as to how you should react to the information:

- *She is the best known for her watercolors of Rocky Mountain scenes.* This is a point in favor of your buying the watercolor you are considering. Now you have to educate yourself about these mountain watercolors, look at as many as you can, find out what the best and worst ones look like, and compare them to the one you are interested in.

- *She did some of her finest work between 1970 and 1980; her worst work was produced between 1955 and 1960.* Find out when the watercolor was painted and act accordingly. If she didn't date her watercolors, find out what characteristics identify her high- and low-point pieces.

- *She tried oil painting for several years but gave it up because she never quite mastered the medium.* You're lucky you aren't considering an oil. If someone offers you one, you should probably pass on it.

- *She had success selling her views of Mt. Ardmore in the mid-1970s, but she mass-produced them during the early 1980s.* If the work you're considering is of Mt. Ardmore and was done in the early 1980s, either pass on it or pay less for it than you would for a more original piece—one that was done before 1980.

- *Mathews paints best in the 20- by 24-inch size range. Her watercolors that measure larger than 25 by 30 inches are not as well done.* Measure the watercolor you like, compare it to others that size and others in different sizes, and act accordingly. If the painting you are evaluating is very large, think about shopping for a smaller one.

A LOOK AHEAD

An additional question to help you evaluate a piece of art is, *What other interesting facts can you find out about the art?* The answer to this question deserves its own chapter—the next one. When evaluating your selections, you need to know as many facts as possible about them, some of which may not be evident from simply researching the artist or viewing and evaluting the art. Particular works of art often stand out above others because of interesting incidental information and are more sought-after by collectors than pieces that lack such information. In Chapter 12 you will learn what kind of information this is and how to go about locating it.

Provenance Is Profit

WHAT PROVENANCE MEANS

You're standing in the Triple-A Fine Arts Gallery considering a Vincent Picasso landscape painting for possible purchase. You have researched the artist, you know the milestones in his career and what subject matters he is recognized for, and you have decided that his art is worth collecting. You have studied a number of his paintings and have concluded that Triple-A's painting is a significant example of his art. You're done with your research. Right?

Not quite.

Additional facts about a work of art—facts that are not obvious from simply viewing the art, viewing other examples of that artist's work, or researching the artist—can significantly affect its value and collectibility. This information, called *provenance,* includes printed, verbal, or other forms of data relating specifically to that work of art's history. Particularly with important art pieces, provenance looms as a major factor in any sales transaction. Though not always obtainable or necessary to possess, when you do have it, you must understand what it means, how to interpret it, and how it influences value.

Provenance can be many things:

A signed statement of authenticity from an art gallery

An exhibition or gallery sticker attached to the art

A sales receipt

A film or recording of the artist talking about the art

An appraisal

Names of previous owners

Letters or papers discussing the art

Newspaper or magazine articles mentioning or illustrating the art

A mention or illustration of the art in a book or exhibit catalogue

Verbal information related by someone familiar with the art

Any data in any form relating directly to the art

Provenance almost always increases the value and desirability of an art piece, because with it, more exists than the art itself. Let's say you own a painting that was originally commissioned by a famous art patron and hung in his personal collection. You own not just another picture but rather one that the renowned Mr. and Mrs. So and So once commissioned and proudly displayed on their living room wall. The fact that your painting was commissioned, owned, and maintained in an exclusive setting makes it, in a sense, a blueblood among paintings.

Proof that your art was actually executed by the artist who signed it is the most basic function of provenance. Even though it is signed and looks authentic, additional documentation provides conclusive evidence that all is right. With the proliferation of forgeries these days, the fact that the art is signed and looks like a recognizable example of an artist's work does not always place it above suspicion. But having good provenance does. For example, you can't dispute a painting's authenticity when you have an exhibit catalogue illustrating the piece or a newspaper article showing the artist standing next to that very painting.

Artists often create provenance on their own and, as a result, influence the futures of individual works of art. Suppose a painter writes in his memoirs or in a letter to a friend that his "View of Slatersby Park" is one of his finest compositions. Even though some art critics may not agree, the Slatersby Park painting becomes exceptional among that artist's output because of the artist's documented opinion.

More unusual examples of provenance include documented incidents of controversy or intrigue. A work of art may have been stolen and recovered fifty years later, or traveled across country in a stagecoach in 1856, or had other adventures befall it. Any revelations that separate an art piece from all others on the market and make it more than just another painting or sculpture or etching or watercolor are what provenance is all about.

Art galleries are well aware of the value of provenance; given two comparable works by the same artist, one with good provenance and one without, the one with provenance will invariably cost more than the one without. Your task is figuring out what good provenance is and how much additional value you should ascribe to what amount and what kind of provenance. You can overpay for inferior provenance the same way you can overpay for inferior art.

Let's examine and then analyze four hypothetical provenances that Triple-A Fine Arts could give you on their Vincent Picasso landscape.

Provenance 1: "We bought the painting privately from an individual who wishes to remain anonymous."

Provenance 2: "This painting hung in an American Art League show at the Boston Museum in 1889 where it won the Hubert D. Thorp prize for excellence in landscape. It was purchased in 1890 by Peter J. Richard, an important New York art collector in his day, and has remained in the Richard family until now. Accompanying the painting is a letter to Peter Richard from Vincent Picasso, dated July 18, 1891, stating that the picture is the 'best landscape he has painted to date.'"

Provenance 3: "The woman who sold us this painting said that the elderly man she bought it from told her that the painting originally belonged to one of Teddy Roosevelt's best friends, a well-known art collector. According to the elderly man, the woman went on to say, it was supposedly one of Teddy's favorite paintings, and he always remarked on it when he visited the collector's home."

Provenance 4: "This painting once hung in the Presidential Suite of the Mayflower Arms Hotel, Detroit's finest accomodation from the 1940s through the early 1970s. From June 14 to June 16, 1968, during their notorious *Rock the Solar System Tour,* the Purple Oranges, Britain's premier psychedelic rock band, stayed in the Presidential Suite. On the night of June 15, 1968, a wild all-night party took place after the concert, and damage to the suite exceeded $20,000. The Vincent Picasso did not escape unharmed. It received a minor tear when Bottomly Scrimpton, lead singer for the Oranges, threw a reproduction Ming table lamp at an obnoxious groupie and missed. The tear has since been expertly repaired. Accompanying the painting is a signed statement from the hotel security guard who was stationed outside the door during the party and copies of Scrimpton's letter of apology to the hotel for destroying the room and the Purple Orange's check for the painting's repair."

How do you as a collector evaluate these four provenances in relation to what you are being asked to pay for the painting? Let's say that a good-quality Vincent Picasso, similar in size, subject matter, and condition to this one, is worth $10,000 with no provenance. The next few paragraphs provide the analysis for each provenance described above.

Provenance 1: This is essentially no provenance at all, and as long as the painting is average-to-good quality and in good condition, the asking price should be $10,000. What you should get with your purchase is a signed statement from Triple-A Fine Arts affirming that the painting is an authentic Vincent Picasso. You should also receive a statement of full money-back guarantee should the authenticity of the painting ever be doubted. This statement will become the painting's provenance.

Provenance 2: You've got an impressive history here. Vincent Picasso considered this painting one of his best, a jury of his peers concurred by awarding him a prestigious award at a national show, and a major private collector agreed by purchasing the piece. That sort of provenance should add at least several thousand dollars to the base price of $10,000, and possibly as much as $8,000 to $10,000 or even more, depending on how many other Vincent Picasso's have those sorts of qualifications. On the high end, if experts believe that this picture is one of Vincent Picasso's greatest efforts, an asking price in excess of $20,000 wouldn't be at all out of line.

Provenance 3: What you're dealing with here is verbal hearsay. This provenance is valid only if the allegations can be investigated and confirmed. Otherwise, assume no provenance—and no increase in price above $10,000—at all.

Unless Triple-A Fine Arts can give you specific names, dates, places, or any other concrete evidence, all you have is gossip that may or may not be true. You need the name of the woman who sold Triple-A the art, the name of the elderly man who gave her the information, and the name of Roosevelt's best friend and well-known collector. As for Teddy's liking the painting, his preferences in art are basically irrelevant because he was a politician, not an art expert.

Be especially careful when presented with gossip or hearsay provenance. Sellers sometimes state it as though it's true and then charge more for the art because of it. No matter how good it sounds or how much of it there is, it's not valid unless you can prove it.

Provenance 4: This is a good story. If you buy the Vincent Picasso and hang it in your living room, being able to relate that bizarre incident while showing it off to your friends does have a dollar value attached to it. Your friends would certainly be more entertained hearing about this moment in rock history than hearing you say, "Look at this wonderful Vincent Picasso landscape I just bought."

Be careful how much you pay for this story, though, because it does not relate to the painting as a work of art, but only to an event, albeit a glamorous one. Assuming that the object of Bottomly's indiscretion is average-to-good quality and in good condition, and that the inflicted damage was minor as stated, the asking price should be increased by a modest amount, perhaps $500 to $1,000 at the very most, above the $10,000 base (unless your mission is to form the definitive collection of paintings damaged in the presence of famous rock stars and you could care less who Vincent Picasso is).

ACQUIRING AND MAINTAINING PROVENANCE

Make every effort to acquire and maintain provenance on all art you own. At the very least, be sure sellers give you signed statements of authenticity and whatever other data they have in their files whenever you buy works of art. Keep individual folders on each work of art you own, and save all pertinent receipts, guarantees, statements by the artists, exhibition catalogues, and anything else relating directly to that art (for additional information about building folders, see Chapter 18). Each folder becomes a part of the art it represents and should remain with that art for all time.

Take what the galleries give you, but at the same time, be aware that they have not necessarily had the time to uncover every minute fact about every work of art they sell. Depending on how fascinated you are with certain artists or art pieces and how industrious you feel, you may want to continue the job of acquiring provenance on your own. The more you find out, the better you understand the history of what you collect, the more sophisticated you become as a collector, and the more your art is worth.

Those of you who truly enjoy ferreting out facts should think of yourselves as detectives out to acquire the complete history of your art from the day it was created right up to the present moment. Trace its existence as far back as you can.

If you are buying contemporary art, the detective work is simple. Get a statement from the gallery and, whenever possible, a statement from the artist specifically relating to the piece in question, and you're done. Add to your file as new developments take place.

You have to work a little harder on older art with vague histories. For art by artists who are still living, contact the artists personally. Send them photographs of what you own, and ask them to comment on it. Request that they supply you with general biographical information about themselves and their careers and, most importantly, any data relating directly to your art. Ask them any questions you have about the art and its origins.

When artists are no longer alive, speak with or write to anyone you know to have been associated with them or their art, and specifically with your art. Locating these people is not always easy. Some collectors use techniques as sophisticated as researching family geneologies, death certificates, property records, probate files, and so on. When you've got the spare time to check these sorts of resources, do so. It's a fascinating procedure, and you never know where you'll end up or what you'll find out.

Previous owners of works of art are another great source of provenance.

Some galleries will give you the names of these people and allow you to contact them. When dealers won't name names (which is often the case), request that they contact those owners themselves, get whatever statements they can, and relate them to you.

A sad commentary on the business of acquiring and documenting provenance on older art is that in many cases, dealers would rather protect their sources than name names of previous owners or tell you what they know about the histories of the art. This dealer reticence comes about because of less scrupulous collectors who learn sellers' names and sometimes attempt to contact those sources themselves to buy from them directly, thereby cutting the original galleries out of the profit picture. Thus, unfortunately, keeping provenance a secret is sometimes just good business sense for the galleries.

At other times, families who sell their art wish to remain anonymous. The dealers whom they work with are not at liberty to reveal names because that was part of the selling arrangement. In any event, you still may be able to locate these people and acquire provenance. Your job is just going to be tougher.

When you are fortunate enough to personally contact a previous owner, an individual who knew the artist well, or anyone else who may have information you need, be aware that they sometimes overlook significant details about the art or never mention them simply because no one has ever asked—so ask. By the way, these are also questions you should ask any dealer selling you art. Sample provenance-gathering questions include the following:

- Where did you purchase this art?

- How long have you owned it?

- Do you know the names of any previous owners?

- Can you identify the subject matter, event, location, or what it represents, or relate any other information about the piece?

- Do you know anything about when, where, why, or how it was produced?

- Do you have or know of any printed materials relating directly to this piece?

- Was it ever in a public exhibition?

- Has anyone ever told you anything interesting about it?

- Do you or did you know the artist personally, and, if so, what was his or her opinion of the art?

- Do you know anyone else who can tell me more? (You take these names and repeat the procedure.)

Additional, more specific questions often arise as you pursue your investigations, but these will get you started.

Researching and acquiring provenance is rewarding in the long run because every discovery you make sends a work of art's value upward. In the same vein, lacking crucial information always results in art being undervalued. Many art dealers have sad tales to tell about art they sold first and discovered important information about later. You are fortunate indeed when you uncover something about an art piece that the person who sold it to you unwittingly overlooked, and the better you get at locating provenance, the greater will be the probability of that happening.

Example 1: Provenance can be conveyed verbally, as well as in writing, which is how I acquired information about a painting by Frederick Judd Waugh, the famous American painter of coastal scenes. The painting's subject, a camouflaged merchant ship on the high seas circa World War I, is not exactly a composition Waugh is famous for and, thus, not exactly a composition collectors seek out for their collections. His fans prefer dramatic coastal scenes with waves crashing on rocks.

The written provenance consisted of the original owner's name and various lifetime addresses on the painting's back. Since I purchased the painting directly from the original owner's estate, I had the opportunity to receive its complete verbal history firsthand from the executor who had been a long-time friend of the family.

According to her, Waugh and the original owner, also an artist, worked for the U.S. government during World War I. Together they researched and developed camouflage configurations for military and merchant ships. While working with Waugh, this artist invented the color battleship gray. The painting had been a gift from Waugh commemorating their relationship.

The unusual subject matter was now understandable and no longer a maverick, unexplainable composition. It fit perfectly into Waugh's career as a historically significant work of art.

I next sent a photograph of the painting to a curator of a naval museum to obtain further information. In his reply, he stated that it was one of the few extant full-color examples of ship camouflage surviving from that time period. This meant that the painting had historic naval significance also. The curator was so impressed by it that he requested that it be donated to the museum and stated that if donated, it would be prominently displayed in the museum's World War I collection.

What initially appeared to be an atypical and, therefore, relatively unpopular picture with collectors took on a whole new meaning with complete provenance. Because of the painting's significance in respect to Waugh's artistic career, as well as to World War I naval history, the tale accompanying the painting made the piece much more attractive to collectors than it would have otherwise been. Without this information, I would have been hard-pressed to place it in any collection.

Example 2: I own a painting by a well-known American artist who was active from the late 1920s through the 1950s. I liked it the moment I saw it, and I decided to buy it for my own collection. The only provenance the painting had was in the form of two tags glued to the painting's back, a museum sticker and the remains of an exhibition sticker.

The complete sticker was from a local museum. The museum had apparently purchased the painting for its collection in the early 1930s but had let the painting go several decades later when the museum decided to go a different direction with its collecting. The fact that a museum once owned a work of art is always a plus point, but what I discovered several years after buying the painting was an even bigger plus point.

One day I was looking through an old handbook of this particular museum's collection, one that had been published in the early 1940s, and found, to my delight, that my painting was one of only several American pictures illustrated. I could conclude from this that the museum had held my painting in special high regard while it owned the work. Not only had the museum considered the painting good enough to purchase, but the museum had also felt that it was one of only a few paintings good enough to be illustrated prominently in the museum's handbook.

I continued to puzzle over the remains of the second tag for several more years, trying to figure out what specific exhibit it was from. I eventually identified the show from the few words remaining on the sticker and, again to my delight, discovered that the show was a major international art exhibition that had been held in the late 1930s. My painting had enjoyed a much more distinguished history than I had initially thought when I bought it. Dollarwise, the painting has also turned out to be worth a lot more than I had initially thought when I bought it.

A LOOK AHEAD

Suppose you have selected a work of art that on the surface appears to qualify for inclusion in your collection and that, according to the research guidelines you have been reading about so far, looks pretty good. Suppose, however, that it has either been damaged in the past, is prone to damage in the future, or, worse yet, is an outright fake. In either of the first two instances, there's a strong possibility you won't want to buy the piece. That possibility becomes a certainty if the art happens to be a forgery.

The next two research chapters concern the topics of damage and forgeries. They are not topics that members of the art community—especially art dealers—enjoy talking about, but they cannot be ignored. Inspecting any selection you make for damage and the possibility that it could be a forgery are the last two steps in your research before you address money issues and, ultimately, decide whether or not to buy.

CHAPTER 13
Damaged Art

Just about all art you see on display in galleries looks to be in perfect condition and looks as though it will last forever. Galleries make every effort to present their art to the public in top viewing condition. But what condition is it really in, and will you have problems with it after you buy it? These are important questions that must be answered before you spend your money.

Think of how long the art you buy will be around. A work of art is not like a car, a television, or any other disposable consumer product that after a few years you throw away or trade in and replace with the latest model. You keep art much longer than you keep other possessions. You may decide to sell it twenty or thirty years down the road. You may own it for fifty years and then pass it down to your children, they may pass it down to *their* children, and so on. Whatever you do with it, you always want it to look its best.

Art dealers and galleries, unfortunately, do far too little to inform and educate their customers about condition, damage, and the consequences of damage. Only at the highest levels of collecting do dealers regularly discuss these topics with their clients. The average art gallery is in business to sell art, and since conversations relating to damage and condition are not usually conducive to making sales, such conversations are simply avoided. Consequently, you have to arm yourself with appropriate knowledge in order to avoid problem art.

A substantial amount of older works of art, for instance, have had problems and been worked on at various points during their lifetimes. Even though they appear to be in original perfect condition, underneath the gloss are histories of damage, condition problems, and repairs.

Contemporary art can have problems too. Just because you buy it brand new does not mean you'll never have to worry about it. Some is not that well constructed and is predisposed to wearing poorly over time. Dealers in contemporary art can document cases of art that substantially deteriorated after only a few years in existence.

For example, several decades ago artists were attracted to certain brands of water-based markers or "water crayons" when they first came onto the market and used them in their art. Within five to ten years the water crayon portions of that art began to fade, and after ten years or so they had faded so seriously that they had either totally changed color or had almost completely disappeared. Artists now know to avoid these crayons.

Contemporary art can also have damage repair, even though the art has only been in existence a short while. A gallery employee may have dropped the art on its corner while transporting it from the artist's studio to the gallery, the piece may have had coffee spilled on it, and so on. Artists can even damage their art in the process of creating it and, rather than starting all over, repair the problems themselves.

Whatever the situation and whatever the art, if what you are considering buying has either had problems in the past or has weaknesses in the present that will lead to problems in the future, you have to know about them. The reason is that *damage decreases value. Art that has damage, is prone to damage, or has suffered damage that has been repaired is worth less than similar art in perfect condition.* It's that simple.

Damage reduces value in another way, also: you must pay to have it fixed. Art that develops problems over time or is damaged while you own it must be repaired, and those repairs cost money. Not only do they cost money, but they often cost a lot of money. Art restoration and conservation is a highly specialized profession, and spending several thousand dollars to restore an art piece is not unusual.

You should not automatically refuse to buy a work of art because it has damage, however. Damaged art is not worthless, as many people believe. For example, I once bought an old, torn, rolled-up canvas at a Texas junk shop for $7.50. The piece looked totally worthless to the shop's owner, but I had no trouble selling it several days later in "as is" condition for $2,500.

The bottom line is this: *Anyone can learn how to evaluate the condition of any work of art on his or her own.* Whether damage has already happened or is yet to come, whether the art looks to be beyond hope or is in pristine condition, the better you are at diagnosing the situation, the fewer problems and added expenses you will have to contend with in the course of your collecting.

LEARNING ABOUT TYPES OF DAMAGE

No matter what kind of art you collect—oil paintings, limited edition prints, watercolors, wood carvings, whatever—you need to learn what specific problems are associated with that type of art. You'll find that for every art form, an entire terminology exists for identification and evaluation of damage. For example, oil paintings can rip, tear, lose paint, or accumulate dirt. Repair procedures include replacing areas of missing paint, mending rips and tears, and removing surface dirt, and the respective technical terms for these repairs are *inpainting, lining,* and *cleaning.*

If you're thinking that the subject of damage is too difficult to understand, relax. You can get a good sense of the basics after only a few hours of instruction. Then, after learning the basics, all you need to do is practice, practice, practice.

The best teachers you can find are repair specialists called "fine-art conservators." No matter what you collect, when it breaks, fades, dents, rips, cracks, or anything else, an art conservator exists who knows exactly how to fix it. These people are trained experts in their particular fields of restoration. You can find out much of what you need to know by visiting and speaking with a conservator or two.

Locate fine-art conservators in your area by checking the Yellow Pages under the heading "Art Restoring." Get additional names by asking art dealers or contacting art museums. Museum references are especially good, and, in fact, many museums operate their own full-time conservation facilities. Some of these institutions even provide formal instruction through occasional seminars or lectures. Also write to the American Institute for Conservation of Historic and Artistic Works to request its membership roster and see whether any of its members are active in your area. The institute's address is: 1400 16th Street NW, Suite 340, Washington, D.C. 20036.

Assemble names from these various sources and speak with the conservators over the phone. Tell them what you collect, and make sure they are experts at restoring it. Anyone you decide to work with should have years of experience and be able to provide you with adequate references. Assuming they are qualified, tell them you are interested in learning about damage and its treatment, and ask whether you can visit them at their studios. Most are happy to spend some time with you and show you firsthand how they work.

While at conservation studios, make sure you do the following:

- See photographs of art in its "before" and "after" condition (you'll quickly realize that expert conservators are truly miracle-workers).

- See restorations in progress.

- Have conservators show you how to identify and diagnose existing unrepaired damage as well as damage that has already been repaired.

- Have them show you specific problems that you could encounter with your art.

- Find out how much each of those problems costs to repair (knowing repair costs comes in very handy if you are ever offered a work of art that is not in perfect condition).

- Learn which types of damage are easy to repair, which are difficult, and which are impossible.

- Pay special attention to learning how to recognize permanent damage. For example, paintings or bronzes that have been cleaned with excessively harsh solvents can have irreplaceable amounts of paint or patinas stripped off their surfaces. The better conservators can hide these sorts of problems, but they can never bring back to the art back the original look that the artists intended it to have. Irreversible damage seriously reduces dollar value and collectibility; avoid it at all costs.

Another way to learn about damage, especially if you want to collect contemporary art, is from artists themselves. Have art galleries, art associations, or museum sale and rental galleries recommend the names of artists who can teach you. As with conservators, speak on the phone first, make appointments, and then visit these artists at their studios. Have them show what to look for in well-made art and how to avoid inferior pieces. Learn the difference between poorly constructed art and art that has been put together with quality materials by artists who know how to use them.

One important warning: Never confuse artists with art conservators. Never ask artists to assess or repair damaged art, even if it is their own. Most artists are totally untrained in proper conservation techniques and procedures. Artists and art conservators are in two entirely different professions. Artists create art; art conservators restore and maintain it.

HOW MUCH DAMAGE IS CONSIDERED ACCEPTABLE?

Experienced art dealers and collectors generally avoid art that has been damaged beyond a certain point. The most serious investment-oriented collectors avoid damage at all costs and prefer to buy art that is in its original, unaltered condition only. The logic is clear: the more damage repair a work of art has, the less it is as the original artist intended it to be and the more it is as the conservator has reconstructed it. In the extreme instance, some art you find for sale has had such severe damage that it is now primarily the work of the repair person and no longer that of the original artist.

Depending on the type of art, certain amounts of damage are considered minor and acceptable by most collectors; larger amounts become increasingly unacceptable and either significantly reduce or totally destroy the value of the art. What those precise amounts are varies according to factors such as age of the art, rarity, importance of the artist, and so on. For example, collectors of fifteenth-century Gothic panel paintings are more liberal in the amount of damage they consider acceptable than are collectors of contemporary watercolors.

Have art dealers—not conservators—teach you what amounts and types of damage are acceptable and not acceptable, how they affect collectibility, and how they affect dollar value. Conservators want to restore art no matter how bad the damage is and are especially eager to get going when damage is severe. Repairing major damage is not only challenging to conservators, but it is also financially rewarding. As a result, conservators tend to downplay the effects of damage on collectibility. Dealers, on the other hand, have substantially less conflict of interest here and give you the straight story.

Two general rules can help you determine how the extent of damage affects the value of any given art piece:

1. *The greater the percentage of damage, the more the value is reduced.* With most art, no damage is best, and 5 percent is minor. Beyond that point, things begin to get a little touchy (unless you happen to be collecting great rarities), and ordinarily 10 percent is about the maximum acceptable amount.

2. *The location of the damage is equally as important as the percentage.* A small amout of damage in the wrong place can destroy a work of art's value.

Consider, for example, a portrait painting of a figure against a black background. Let's say it's in perfect condition except for severe damage to one eye. Eyes are usually the most important details in a portrait and are crucial to understanding and appreciating the picture as a whole. When one eye has to be entirely repainted by a conservator, the essence of the painting is substantially altered and possibly even lost. That new eye will never look the same as the original, and thus the painting's value is markedly decreased. If, however, that same percentage of damage is to the plain black background behind the figure and the rest of the painting is perfect, overall value is reduced only slightly.

For every type of art that exists, a system also exists for inspecting and determining the condition of that art. You inspect oil paintings a certain way, watercolors a certain way, sculptures a certain way, and so on. Whether you buy period or contemporary art, learn proper procedures for what you collect and always follow them before you buy. No matter what you collect, the general pointers given below will be of help.

Begin Any Condition Inspection By Asking the Seller for a Full Condition Report. When repairs have been made in the past, have the seller show you exactly where they are located and how extensive they are. Sometimes— not nearly often enough, but the practice is becoming more common— conservators attach descriptions of their completed work to the art. This information includes what repairs have been made, how they were made, and what chemicals or other materials were used in the process.

Inspect the Art Using the Techniques You Learn From Art Conservators and Dealers. Always do this yourself, no matter how much information the seller gives you. You are the buyer; you deserve to examine all selections fully before buying.

How do you inspect for damage? Very closely. If you need a magnifying glass, buy one. Don't be embarrassed to study the most minute details of an art piece. That scratch, chip, or dent may be small, and that repaired tear may not be visible from more than two feet away, but they are there just the same, and they affect the value of the art.

Buy Any Specialized Tools You May Need to Help Check for Damage. For example, a hand-held ultraviolet light is often used to inspect for damage repairs on old oil paintings, textiles, works on paper, glass, and ceramics. Make sure you learn how to use whatever equipment you buy before you try to use it to examine art you are considering. As always, it is best to have fine-art conservators, art dealers, or other experts train you in proper inspection techniques and equipment use.

Whenever You See Any Aspect of an Artwork That You Don't Fully Understand or That Looks Suspicious, Ask About It. Whether it turns out to be damage repair or structural weakness or the way the artist meant the art to be, satisfy yourself fully before buying. If you have any doubts whatsoever about a piece, have a conservator examine it independently *before you buy.*

Be Wary of Sellers Who Give Vague Answers to Your Questions Regarding Condition or, Worse Yet, Discourage Condition Examinations Altogether. Your best option is not to patronize galleries where you have experienced such treatment. Unless you are expert at inspecting condition yourself and are willing to take the necessary risks, do your buying elsewhere.

Whenever Possible, Get a Written Condition Report and an Accompanying Guarantee That if the Condition Is Not As It Has Been Represented You Will Receive a Complete Refund of the Purchase Price. This guarantee protects you from sellers who deliberately misrepresent the condition of their art. Misrepresentation doesn't happen often, but it does happen.

MAINTAINING YOUR ART

Few people ever think of asking how to care for their art once they own it. They hang it on the wall or place it on its pedestal and forget about it. Years later, they discover problems and end up having to pay costly repair or cleaning bills.

Art has care and maintenance instructions just like anything else. Have dealers and conservators show you the best way to maintain your art. For additional instruction, read *Collecting and Care of Fine Art,* by Carl David (New York, Crown Publishers, 1981). Also, write to the American Institute for Conservation of Historic and Artistic Works for advice and ask if the institute can recommend any additional publications (the address was provided earlier in this chapter).

The general rules for proper care and maintenance of fine art are as follows:

- *Avoid excessive dryness or humidity.*

- *Avoid exposure to direct sunlight.*

- *Avoid temperature extremes.* Average room temperature is best.

- *Avoid exposure to smoke from either fireplaces or tobacco.* If you have a problem with smoke, protect your art under glass or plexiglass to save costly cleaning bills later.

- *Protect art that has many intricate exposed edges or surfaces by placing it under glass or plexiglass.* Years of dirt and dust accumulation on highly detailed surfaces can be costly, time-consuming, and sometimes even impossible to remove. Regular dusting does not necessarily keep dirt from accumulating on this sort of art.

- *Frame art using only top-quality materials, and have professional framers do the work.* Inferior frames, mats, and other mountings can damage art over time.

- *Never alter your art in any way for either protection or display purposes.* For example, never cut down a painting in order to fit it into a smaller frame, never drill holes in a sculpture in order to mount a nameplate, and so on. Alterations severely reduce collectibility and dollar value.

- *Check your art closely from time to time to make sure that no problems are developing.* Catch things early, before they get too serious, in order to avoid expensive repair bills.

- *Never clean art using any chemicals (bleach, ammonia, window cleaner, paint thinner, furniture polish, and so on).* Use nothing more than a feather duster or a light dry cloth (unless you are instructed otherwise by a dealer or conservator). Clean on a regular basis to prevent dust and dirt buildup.

- *Never attempt to repair art yourself.* Art dealers and art conservators can tell you horror stories about amateur repair attempts that reduced valuable art to worthless junk.

- *Employ only qualified fine-art conservators to treat your art—not artists, not your next-door neighbor who happens to be handy at repairing things, not any other amateurs who think they know how to fix it.* If you damage your art or it becomes dirty with age, take it to at least two conservators and compare opinions on what needs to be done, how treatment will be performed, and how much it will cost; then get the work done. Cutting corners by employing semiprofessionals or amateurs may save you a few dollars in the short run, but such an approach could jeopardize the value of your art in the long run.

Example 1: I once attended an art opening for an artist who, at that time, had been painting for about ten years. He was showing a series of large paintings, priced between $3,000 and $5,000 each, done using a new technique he had recently developed. What was on the canvases was not really paint, but rather a heavily textured malleable substance that felt more like soft putty. The art *looked* great, but I had several strong reactions to it, all negative.

First, the paintings were unprotected. The slightest touch made an impression in the surface texture. Second, keeping the art clean would be extremely difficult. Even a light dusting would alter the putty-like surface.

These problems could at least be avoided by protecting the paintings under glass or plexiglass, but what if these paintings ever got damaged? Would conservators have the technology to repair them? Could they even *be* repaired, or would conservators never be able to reconstruct damaged areas?

As if those worries weren't enough, I looked into the future and tried to imagine what would become of these pictures. Would gravity take its toll and eventually pull this substance down and off the canvases? Would it dry in five or ten or one hundred years and leave great cracks or shrunken areas?

The artist had apparently not considered any of these potential consequences. To me, spending thousands of dollars on one of these pictures seemed like something between an incredible risk and a complete waste of money. Sure, the art looked great at the moment of the opening, but more goes into creating art than producing temporary good looks. It must be made to permanently survive intact and retain the characteristics it was originally meant to have.

Example 2: Even standard household cleaners and polishes can destroy works of art. A collector I know completely removed the finish from a $1,500 metal sculpture simply by dusting it several times a month with a nationally advertised furniture polish and dust remover. The dustings gradually removed the finish along with the dust in a process which occurred so slowly that the collector did not realize what he had done until it was too late. The sculpture is now worth only several hundred dollars.

Example 3: Early in my career I bought a landscape painting that I thought was in perfect condition. It was a little dirty, so I decided to have my conservator do a light surface cleaning. He took one look at it and immediately told me that something was wrong.

At first, he wasn't sure what the problem was, but after studying the painting for a few minutes he said he thought the sky looked a little funny. To him, it looked to be painted in a style different from of the rest of the painting. He proceeded to chemically remove a small area of the sky, and, sure enough, the painting's original sky was underneath. Somebody had completely painted it over.

My painting now needed to have the entire false sky removed in addition to the light surface cleaning. The surface cleaning would have cost $200 at most. Just to remove the sky would cost an additional $1,500, and, once it was off, any damage to the original sky, if it was not in perfect condition, would cost more hundreds of dollars to repair. My painting was not worth restoring, and I ended up selling it for less than what I had paid. I now know how to recognize when portions of paintings have been painted over, believe me.

A LOOK AHEAD

Related to condition inspection is forgery detection. Both involve close physical examination of art and both are often performed simultaneously. Now more than ever, it is necessary for collectors to be fluent about the nature and detection of forgeries—the darkest side of art research. Chapter 14 will start you on your way to such fluency.

CHAPTER 14
Forgers and Forgeries

Ask any art dealer whether he or she has ever been taken advantage of by art forgers, and you'll find that the answer is almost always yes. Art is faked on a constant basis, and anyone can be victimized at any time. The best forgers are skilled enough to fool even experienced professionals.

Forgers provide whatever collectors are looking for. Forgers know which artists sell well in the marketplace, what their art looks like, and how they sign. After carefully selecting works of art that have just the right look, forgers give those pieces fake signatures or documentations, and the deception begins.

Art collecting is more popular than ever, and, as a result, forgers are enjoying a great deal of success. These criminals have risen to the occasion and are hard at work keeping up with the increased demand. Now more than ever you take your chances when you assume that just because a work of art is signed or otherwise stated to be a given artist's work, all is in order. You've got to "look under the hood" and confirm for yourself that the art is being truthfully represented.

This does not mean that you should run around paranoid, never believing a single word dealers tell you. The great majority of art is authentic; the great majority of sellers are honest. Fakes, however, are a fact of the art business, and the less you know about them, the more likely you are to end up with one in your collection.

No matter where you buy art, you should be concerned about forgeries. Whether you shop exclusively at established galleries and are protected by money-back arrangements or you decide to explore alternative avenues for acquiring art, you could end up purchasing a forgery. However, you adventurers who get the urge to wander outside established gallery settings, as many collectors do once they get their feet wet, should be especially concerned. Flea markets, estate sales, local auctions, antique shops, traveling art shows, and less established galleries are great places to look for art bargains, but they are also the most likely places to end up buying art forgeries.

No matter what your budget, you should be concerned about forgeries. You've probably heard occasional news stories about collectors being taken for millions of dollars by forgery rings or about a valuable original being removed from the wall of a museum and a worthless copy hung in its place. Tales like these make great entertainment, but they're not characteristic of the techniques and methods of the average forger—the forger whose work you could well encounter as you go about your day-to-day collecting. Art forgery is widespread and routine, and it affects art at all price levels, not only at the level of the highly expensive pieces. Don't think you're safe just because you're not buying Picassos or Van Goghs.

Be aware of the following three truths about forgers and forgeries:

1. Forgeries are everywhere.

2. Forgers fake all types of art.

3. Forgers forge and sell art in all price ranges.

You or anyone else can take certain precautions to help identify and avoid questionable works of art, but a strong word of warning is in order here. *As long as you're unsure of your ability to spot fakes, stick with established dealers who provide money-back guarantees of authenticity.* Buying art on your own without expert advice is always a risky proposition. Regardless of those risks, however, some of you are going to take chances anyway, so the balance of this chapter offers some tips and hints that might help you avoid getting had.

KNOW YOUR ARTISTS

No matter where you buy or what you are buying, the number-one rule is to know your artists. An artist's style, subject matters, colors, favorite media, signature, and other qualities of his or her art are as unique and individual as fingerprints or handwriting. Knowing what an artist's work looks like and how that artist signs protects you from buying a fake that happens to have his or her name on it.

The great majority of transactions involving forgeries could be instantly eliminated if only buyers took time to learn more than artists' names before heading out into the open market. Whenever you are offered art by an artist whose work you don't know all that well, get the advice of experts, locate known examples by that artist, and compare them to what you are being offered. Always do this *before* you buy.

HOW FORGERS SELL

Forgers have to sell what they produce, and they do so in a variety of ways. They victimize art dealers, private collectors, antiques shop owners, flea marketers, art gallery owners, estate liquidators, and other outlets. Some even hawk their wares through the classified ads of local papers. The most innocent-looking sale can have forgeries in it. Don't think you're safe just because you are buying from a little old lady who lives out in the country, far from big-city evils.

You or anyone else can come face to face with someone intentionally selling fakes. These people know how to back you into a corner and limit your options in terms of deciding whether or not to buy. Here are several ways they work:

- They prevent you from doing research by claiming they don't have time to wait.

- They insist that the art has been handed down in their families or that it was purchased directly from the artists, but they don't allow you any time for verification.

- They distract you from normal research procedures by making you think you're getting great bargains.

- They tell you they have other buyers just waiting to buy if you don't.

Forgers say whatever is necessary to fool you. Watch out when any aspect of a selling situation seems out of the ordinary.

Forgers also consign to auctions. They usually victimize local or regional houses that don't employ full-time art experts, but even major houses get fooled from time to time. As with art dealers and antiques shops that inadvertently buy and then sell occasional forgeries, auctions also innocently pass them on to private collectors. Auctions protect themselves with disclaimers, though—everything is sold "as is," buyer beware. This situation makes auction buying, especially at small, transient or less established firms, a risky venture for novice collectors. If you make a mistake *you* are responsible, not the auction house. (You can read more about auction buying in Chapter 19, "Action at the Auction.")

LEARNING TO DETECT FORGERIES

Learning to inspect art for signs that it has been tampered with is similar to learning how to evaluate it for damage, condition, and durability problems. You should contact the appropriate experts—namely dealers, curators, and conservators—and ask them to teach you what to look for. Each specific type of art has a specific system of checking for authenticity, and you can learn that system from experts in those fields.

In order to distinguish a work that is totally original from one that has been manipulated in some way, you have to become familiar with every aspect of the art, not just the image or the subject. You have to know it from top to bottom; inside and out; back, front, and sides. With a painting, for example, you look not only at the composition and signature but also at the framing, the back of the picture, the sides, the gallery stickers, the tags, writings or markings on any other parts of the painting or the frame, and so on. Every detail about a work of art is a clue to whether or not it is right.

Finding authentic originals to study and learn from is never a problem. The hard part (and the important part) is finding forgeries to compare with those originals. Dealers are sometimes reluctant to show forged works, but many have one or two put away in the back rooms of their galleries or can tell you where to go to see them. Examine forgeries firsthand whenever possible and see exactly how and where they have been tampered with. Get dealers to show and explain them to you at every opportunity.

Other ways to learn about forgeries include attending seminars sponsored by art galleries or museums and reading about famous forgers and how they operate. For example, one major American museum recently exhibited forgeries next to originals so that patrons and collectors could compare and contrast their different qualities. For you forgery fans who are intrigued by the topic and would like to do some further reading, the two best basic books are *The Art of the Forger,* by Christopher Wright (New York, Dodd Mead, 1984), and *The Forger's Art,* edited by Denis Dutton (Berkeley, University of California Press, 1983).

Also contact the International Foundation for Art Research. This nonprofit organization deals exclusively with art theft, fraud, and fakes. If you want up-to-the-minute news on the state of the art world's underbelly, subscribe to the foundation's publication, IFAR Reports. Write to: International Foundation for Art Research, 46 East 70th Street, New York, NY 10021.

SPOTTING THE ART AND CRAFT OF FORGERY

Almost all forgeries involve manipulation of a signature. An old signature may be altered or removed and a new signature added, or if the art is unsigned to begin with, a new signature may simply be added. Sometimes the art is actually by the artist whose signature has been added—it was unsigned to begin with and was signed by a third party to increase its value—but this makes no difference. It's still a faked signature, and whenever someone other than the original artist signs a piece of art, you are dealing with a forgery.

Correct Signatures Should Look Natural and Unforced, Be Located Where the Artist Customarily Signs, Be In the Color or Manner the Artist Customarily Signs In, and Match In Other Particulars Such as How *t*'s Are Crossed and *i*'s Are Dotted. Checking a signature against an example in a reference book or signature dictionary sometimes helps, but just because the two look identical doesn't mean you automatically assume the one you're checking is right. The forger could have copied from the exact same reference you're using. You've got to go further and study multiple examples firsthand from a variety of sources, preferably the artworks themselves.

Beware of Pencil or Pen Signatures On Paintings, Works On Paper, or Sculptures (Unless This Is How the Artists Regularly Signed). Forgers who are not very good at using brushes and paints often sign pictures this way. With sculptures, writing fake signatures is much easier than carving or casting them. Even when such signatures are authentic, serious dealers and collectors still tend to avoid them. They prefer signatures in the medium of the composition: oil on oil, watercolor on watercolor, gouache on gouache, wood carved into wood, metal sculpture signatures cast in the metal, and so on.

Make Sure Pencil or Ink Drawings Are Signed In the Identical Pencil or Ink Used to Make the Drawings. Sometimes a discrepancy between inks or leads is obvious; other times it is only visible under a magnifying glass or jeweler's loupe. The slightest difference between the ink or lead used on the signature and that used on the drawing usually means trouble. Settle for nothing less than a perfect match.

Suspect Signatures Scratched into Dried Paint or Sculpted Surfaces. In these cases you notice small chips or other irregularities around the lines forming the names. Usually these are visible with the naked eye, but, once again, magnifying names is a good idea. Scratched names are frequently added well after the art has been completed, not immediately after as is normal procedure for the artist.

Check to See That Names Blend Naturally with the Rest of the Art. Signatures that look out of place may have been added recently. For example, a name on an older painting or sculpture may look fresh and new, a name may be in a color that seems out of place with the rest of the colors in the art, and so on.

Sometimes Original Signatures Are Erased or Painted Out and Replaced with Different Ones. Examine places where artists sign (usually the lower corners of pictures, bases of sculptures, margins of graphic works, and so on) and see whether attempts have been made to alter or remove old names. Small areas differing in brushstroke, color, or texture give this away.

Make Sure Names Are Spelled Correctly. Surprisingly, this does happen! Artists themselves have been known to misspell, but if you encounter a misspelling you are most likely viewing a forger's error.

Watch out for paintings, watercolors, and prints that are unsigned on the front but signed elsewhere—perhaps on the back of the canvas, artist board, paper, or stretcher bars. These pictures may be genuine, but, once again, unless an artist is known for signing in locations other than on the front, watch out.

Art That Is Only Initialed as Opposed to Fully Signed Can Present Problems. For one thing, forging initials is easier than forging entire names. For another, art executed and initialed by minor artists can be misrepresented as being by famous artists who just happen to have the same initials. In such a case, the forger leaves the art exactly as it is. All he or she does is find a good, collectible name to match with the initials and then claim that the work was done by the more collectible artist.

Certain Artists Have Names That Are Easily Copied and Often Faked. Find out who those artists are from dealers and fellow collectors. Be especially careful when you are presented with art signed by those artists.

Some Dealers Have Reputations for Handling Forgeries or Forging Art Themselves. You learn who to watch out for only after you get well involved with collecting. Art dealers and other art business insiders do not name names and incriminate people until after they get to know and trust you.

Some Forgers Do Not Sign Names, but Instead They Photocopy Artist Listings from Reference Books and Attach Them to the Backs of Unsigned Pictures, to the Bases of Unsigned Sculptures, and So On. The presentation may look official and indisputable, but no signature is no signature, and that's that. Additional proof of authenticity is required.

A Variation on the Photocopied Listing Ruse Is the Fabrication of Official-Looking Documents or Certificates That Appear to Authenticate Unsigned Works of Art. Once again, the art is still unsigned, and unless these authentications are from respected experts or authorities, be very careful (of course, these documents and names can be forged, too). Have the art reevaluated by experts you know and trust before you decide to buy.

Beware of Unsigned Works of Art Which Identify the Artists Only By Nameplates on the Frames of Paintings, the Bases of Sculptures, and So On. Anyone can purchase beautiful custom brass nameplates and have them engraved in any manner. No matter how impressive the plate, the art is still unsigned, and you need more proof.

Framing, Backing, Glass, or Special Mountings and Display Cases Are Sometimes Used to Disguise Forgeries and Make Close Inspection Difficult. Sealing the back of a picture, for example, may hide a new canvas that has been painted to look old. Enclosing a bronze in a plexiglass case may make it difficult to tell whether it is an original or a recast. If you have questions, request permission to remove art from its frame or case and examine it at close range.

Pay Attention to the Asking Price. Forgers often entice victims by offering big-name art at extremely cheap prices. When the price seems to be a bargain and the seller is well aware of this, the reason could be that the art is a forgery. Sellers are rarely inclined to give art away at bargain prices unless something is seriously wrong with it.

Watch Out for "Verbal" Forgeries. This is the easiest way of all to fake authenticity. All a seller has to do is show you an unsigned work of art and insist that a particular artist did it or that it looks remarkably like the work of that artist. Unless that seller is a recognized and accepted authority on the artist and is willing to put all statements into writing along with an unconditional money-back guarantee, avoid the art.

In Extreme Cases, Everything Is Faked. A nameplate is added, a special pedestal or frame is constructed, a signature is forged, fake gallery or exhibition stickers are added, and a date or title or inscription is written or glued to the back or base. Do not assume that just because so many details point to the authorship of a particular artist that the art is automatically genuine.

You see that forgers manipulate in many ways, so thoroughly inspect all details on any art you are unsure about. Never shortcut the inspection procedure; get outside expert opinions whenever you have questions. And don't try to be too clever, especially when you're buying out there in the wilds. That bargain you think you are sneaking past some unsuspecting dealer may well be bogus.

SOME METHODS FOR CHECKING PAINTINGS

Inspecting signatures on paintings in darkened surroundings under ultraviolet light is a relatively common practice. Briefly, forged signatures sometimes "fluoresce" or appear to float above the rest of the composition. Art dealers, conservators, and other experts can teach you how to examine art under ultraviolet light.

Infrared rays are also used to inspect paintings. This technique, known as *infrared reflectometry,* involves the use of a special video camera that transmits pictures of an infared exposed painting onto a television screen. Infrared reflectometry can detect previous restorations, paint inconsistencies, and sometimes even act like an x-ray to identify paintings under paintings.

Pocket microscopes sometimes come in handy when examining paintings. As paintings age, the paint tends to shrink, and surface cracks eventually appear. Many cracks are so small that they are not visible to the naked eye. These "microcracks" are visible under microscopes, however, and studying the cracks around a signature helps to determine whether that name is as old as the painting itself or whether it has been recently added (forged). Old original signatures "microcrack" right along with the rest of the paint. Newly added names, on the other hand, do not show cracks, and the new signatures appear to rest over the original microcracks. Have professionals show you how to use hand-held microscopes and how to recognize signature problems before you go out diagnosing paintings on your own.

Chemical detection and examination techniques also exist for identifying forged or tampered with paintings. Solubility tests, for example, have to do with how quickly paint dissolves in certain chemical solutions. Basically, paint that dissolves quickly in mild solvents tends to be new. Paint that dissolves slowly is older. For example, if a paint sample from a signature that is supposed to be 100 years old dissolves easily, that signature could be fake. *Never* do any sort of solubility testing on your own—only expert conservators know how to do it properly.

Pigment identification is another test conservators use to identify problem art. Usually, this is done using a technique called *polarizing microscopy*, which involves studying the way paint samples look under a microscope when exposed to polarized light. If a painting is signed and dated 1889, for example, but polarizing microscopy reveals that the signature contains a pigment that wasn't invented until 1930, something's clearly not quite right. Another situation in which authenticity could be questioned is when signature pigments don't match those of the rest of the painting. Once again, this sort of testing must be performed only by qualified professionals.

FORGED LIMITED EDITION PRINTS

Prints are easier to doctor than most other works of art because only pencil signatures need to be added. Forged signatures on prints are also more difficult to detect than are those on other types of art because just about anyone with writing skills and larcenous intent can practice signing a particular name 500 or 1,000 times and get pretty good at it. Forgers who forge print signatures do not have to worry about mixing special paint colors, camouflaging existing signatures, matching special pencil leads, and so on. A few seconds with an ordinary pencil is all that's necessary.

Forgers manipulate prints in several ways, the main one being that they add signatures to unsigned prints. Unlike paintings and other works of art, prints with fake signatures are usually the work of the artists whose names they bear; the print is authentic, but the signature is not. So don't believe, for example, that just because an authentic Picasso, Chagall, or Dali print happens to have what appears to be Picasso's, Chagall's, or Dali's signature on it that these artists actually signed them.

Photographic reproductions of well-known prints are sometimes marketed as hand-pulled originals. In such cases, the prints are either hand-signed and sold as originals or they are left unsigned, "verbally" doctored, and sold as originals. Photographic reproductions of prints are worth only a few dollars each at best, no matter how famous the artists are. For example, a signed original Chagall lithograph might be worth $30,000; that same lithograph unsigned might be worth $5,000; and a photo reproduction of that lithograph would be worth about $20.

Have print experts show you how to recognize the difference between reproductions and originals. The great majority of reproductions are composed of dot-matrix patterns—much like newspaper illustrations—while originals are not. When you magnify reproductions, you see dot patterns. When you magnify originals, you don't. Whenever you have any doubts, check with experts other than the sellers *before buying.*

FORGED SCULPTURES

The most common problem encountered when buying sculptures is identifying whether you are being offered a reproduction or an original. Most art dealers tell you when they are offering repros, but others simply say nothing. If you don't ask, they don't volunteer the information.

Another problem with sculptures is known as posthumous casting. This means that a sculpture is cast from an artist's prototype after the artist has died. Often this is done without skilled supervision and without the knowledge of the artist's descendants. As with reproductions, these castings are then marketed as originals.

A recent development in sculpture forgery is the replacing of minor names on sculptures with those of major artists during an actual casting process. In this forgery approach, bronzes by minor sculptors are recast from old castings, but before the recasting, original signatures are covered over and replaced with more important names. This used to happen only on rare occasions, but it is now becoming more prevalent.

Example 1: I've bought forgeries. In fact, I've bought them on several different occasions, each time under different circumstances. I'll recount three incidents of who took me, what I bought, and how I got taken, or, as I prefer to think of it, how I took myself.

First Incident *Who took me:* The owner of a small-town antiques shop. *What I bought:* Two paintings by well-known American artists.

How I got taken: The paintings were way underpriced, and I was more interested in getting bargains and maximizing my profit than examining the paintings and requesting provenance. I asked the seller no questions about the art because I didn't want him to suspect that he was selling so cheaply (clever me). I figured I was safe because this fellow was way out in the country, he appeared to know little about art, and he seemed like an innocent antiques dealer who just happened to have a couple of paintings hanging on his walls. He turned out to know a lot more than he let on. He was a crack forger who had sold many fakes during his career. I did not discover that my paintings had forged signatures until well after this dealer had closed up his shop and moved on. He left no forwarding address.

Second incident *Who took me:* A local art dealer. *What I bought:* A small painting by a well-known American artist.

How I got taken: I was familiar with the style and signature of this artist. At a glance, all looked right. The painting matched perfectly in both style and signature, so I felt no need to examine it in depth. When I got home, I realized that the artist's name was spelled wrong. I then took a look at the name under ultraviolet light and it "floated," as some fake signatures do. I returned the painting the next day, and the dealer gladly refunded my money. I later found out that he had a long-standing reputation for forging signatures. This was an excellent forgery; I still think about how good it was, except for that minor error.

Third incident *Who took me:* A vendor at a local flea market. *What I bought:* Three small paintings by an early twentieth-century Dutch artist.

How I got taken: I was unfamiliar with this artist and had never seen any examples of his work. I asked the seller how he knew the paintings were authentic. He gave me a detailed story about how he had purchased them in Europe from a reputable dealer and assured me that they were absolutely genuine. I believed him and bought the paintings. I then offered them to a major art gallery and was immediately told that they were fakes and that a European dealer/forger had recently been selling them throughout the area. The next day, while relating the incident to another gallery owner, he told me that he had brought the same three paintings from the flea marketer several months earlier and had returned them after discovering that they were not authentic. I did the same, and I'm sure this flea marketer continued reselling those paintings until he found a victim who kept them.

Example 2: Several years ago, word was out among dealers that a certain art restorer was faking signatures. His primary outlet was a small local auction house where he would put as many as five to ten forgeries through every sale. Dealers and experienced collectors knew which pictures to avoid, but no one had enough evidence to accuse the man directly and inform the auction house owner about what was happening. In the meantime, plenty of unsuspecting "bargain hunters" with no idea what they were bidding on were getting taken for hundreds and sometimes thousands of dollars per forgery.

I did occasional business with this restorer and, on one occasion, sold him a pleasant nineteenth-century landscape signed indistinctly in the lower right corner of the canvas. Some months later, the picture appeared for sale at the local auction house. The original signature had been removed and replaced with a new and more important one in the opposite corner. I saw the painting at the auction preview and had all the proof I needed to inform the auction house about what was going on.

The good news is that this restorer was permanently barred from consigning to that auction. The bad news is that he remains active as a forger. His work still shows up at other local auctions and antiques shops, but he now covers his tracks. He no longer consigns items himself but instead has others do it for him; also, he never consigns too many items in one place.

Accusing, arresting, and convicting forgers is almost impossible. In order to prosecute someone for forging, that person must be caught in the act of forging; that is, someone must actually *witness* the signings firsthand. Keeping forged art off the market is harder yet. Art will always be forged. The responsibility for detecting and avoiding bogus art lies with you, the collector. Make sure you protect yourself.

A LOOK AHEAD

This completes your basic course in art and artist research. At this point, assuming the initial selections you made during the course of your Part II art gallery explorations are still under consideration, you have only one additional detail to evaluate: the asking prices. If you're like the great majority of collectors, you want to pay a fair and reasonable price for whatever art you buy. Part IV, the last part of this book, shows you how to determine what that fair price is and then explains how to go about buying art once you have made that determination.

Part IV: Buy

The relationship between art and money has become increasingly complex in recent years. Art prices are no longer set in a straightforward manner, and fewer and fewer collectors buy what they do purely for decorative purposes. These days, whenever the word "art" is mentioned in conversation, you can bet that the word "investment" won't be far behind. It is unfortunate that for so many collectors, art appears to be going the way of stocks, bonds, and pork bellies, but that does not mean that you must blindly follow suit. You can still approach art collecting with love, passion, and common sense.

The final and, in many ways, most important step in collecting art is understanding the selections that you are considering for purchase in terms of what you are being asked to pay for them and, in the end, buying them if they seem acceptable from all aspects discussed in this book. Do not confuse this process with procuring art for "investment" purposes. The goal of Part IV is merely to assure your fair treatment in the marketplace, nothing more. You accomplish this by acquiring a working knowledge of the general relationship of art to money, getting instruction in evaluating specific asking prices, and learning how to properly consummate art business transactions.

CHAPTER 15

The Economics of Art: An Introduction

Art is a commodity. This statement sounds crude, but it's the truth. Art is bought, sold, and traded in the marketplace much like all other articles of commerce. The fact that money changes hands as art moves between artists and dealers and collectors requires that it be examined, at least at some point, from a purely economic standpoint.

Fine art never starts out as just another thing to buy and sell. Its creation is one of the most personal and individual forms of expression known to humankind. It is the product of an artist's confrontation with, reaction to, and interpretation of life and the specific reality in which he or she lives. But the moment a work of art is completed and leaves the artist's studio, it becomes subject to many of the same laws of buy and sell, and supply and demand, as do other hard goods.

To begin with, let's examine two fundamental truths about the art economy:

1. *Some art is worth more than other art.* Certain works of art provide us with more to look at and think about than do other works of art. These certain works may be historically significant, unique in special ways, the products of pure genius, masterworks by great artists, and so on. Collectors pay more for art with such distinguished characteristics than they do for art that lacks depth, significance, or quality.

2. *Art prices can fluctuate over time.* The values of works of art do not necessarily remain constant over time. Changes in value can be the result of general outside forces such as taste, fashion, or overall economic climate. They can also be the consequence of progressions of events within particular artists' careers.

Dealers and collectors respond to these two phenomena by evaluating dollars and cents as well as aesthetics when they buy. Beauty, visual appeal, and critical acceptance are considered in varying degrees right alongside asking price, demand in the marketplace, and projected financial performance over time. Some individuals place major emphasis on the money aspects of art; others buy, sell, and collect primarily because they love art and don't care that much about money.

No buying pattern is right or wrong, better or worse. There are pure speculators and pure art lovers—and everything in between—buying, selling, trading, and otherwise transacting art according to their own personal feelings and beliefs about art and dollars.

The total of all this transacting results in what can be called the art economy or art market. Whether a piece of art involved in the market ends up in a museum, in a private collection, in an historical society, in a dusty attic or damp basement, or in the garbage, anytime it transfers from owner to owner, dollar values are set according to certain criteria, and money in some form or other—cash, trade, tax-deductible donation, etc.—changes hands (unless the art is an outright gift to someone). However, before learning what these criteria are and how to apply them to what you want to collect, you need to know some basic facts about the relationship of art to money.

THE LIQUIDITY OF ART

The first and foremost truth about art and its relation to money is that art is not immediately liquid. Repeat: *Art is not immediately liquid.* You cannot simply cash in the art you own like stocks, bonds, or other investments whenever you need or feel like having money. Selling art takes time, sometimes months, and that's longer than many people who want quick cash are able to wait.

Art is more like real estate in terms of liquidity. If, for example, you put your house up for sale at a certain price, you have to wait until the right person comes along and buys it. You may get lucky and sell it quickly, or it may stay on the market unsold for months.

Certain art dealers and art galleries would like to make you think that art is instantly convertible to cash, but no matter what sort of profit-laden tales they tell, you take your financial life into your own hands when you "invest" in art with the idea that you can convert it back to cash at any given moment.

Many people are not aware of how *un*liquid art is. They don't realize that art galleries have to wait for quite a while for customers to come in and buy what is for sale. A small percentage of art does sell immediately, but the great majority takes weeks, months, sometimes even years to sell. Art galleries will tell you that, on the average, a work of art takes between two and eight months to sell.

As for auctions, the art sales you read about in the papers may seem immediate—as if sellers are cashing in their art instantly—but that's not true at all. With auctions, you often have to wait six months or longer between the time you notify the auction house that you're interested in selling and the day you finally get your check in the mail. At worst, your art may not sell at all, in which case the auction house returns it to you and you have to try and sell it all over again somewhere else.

Art is immediately liquid in one sense, though not a pleasant one. Most art is convertible to cash within a week or so, but, unfortunately, you have to accept whatever buyers are willing to pay you at the moment you decide to sell. If you must have immediate cash you have no time to solicit or wait for reasonable offers. For example, if you have one week to sell a sculpture you paid $5,000 for and the best offer you get is $750, that's it. You either sell the sculpture or keep it.

The bottom line: *Spend only discretionary capital on art.* Never tie up emergency funds or money you need for day-to-day expenses to buy art. That's an extremely high-risk proposition.

UNIQUE ASPECTS OF THE ART ECONOMY

The art economy may resemble other economies in the way sales are transacted and the way works of art change hands, but it is very different in several important ways.

With art, no obvious relationship exists between price and product. Take, for example, three paintings that are identical in size, amount of paint on the canvas, cost of materials, amount of time to paint, and all other physical characteristics. The only dissimilarity is that each was executed by a different artist. Even though all else is equal, one painting may be priced at $200, one at $2,000, and the last at $200,000. Whereas the price differential between a Hyundai and a Rolls Royce, for example, is based on concrete variables like manufacturing time, amount of labor involved in production, quality of materials, and end-product performance, with art this is not necessarily the case.

No formal laws, standards, or regulations exist for pricing art. Those selling art can set whatever prices they want for whatever reason they want on whatever art they have for sale. A seller can ask $100 for a work of art or $100,000 for it. Any price is legal, as long as he or she makes no special claims about the art and does not misrepresent it in any way.

Art is not subject to quality controls. No law requires artists to have produced art for a certain period of time or to have reached a certain level of accomplishment before being allowed to sell their art (at whatever price they decide to sell it for). Anyone can claim to be an artist, anyone can create anything and call it art, and anyone can sell it.

What does all this mean? It means that you've got to be aware of the unique aspects of the art market and take them into consideration every time you evaluate art asking prices. Explaining the price difference between Painting A and Painting B, for instance, may not be as easy as explaining price differences between a Rolls Royce and a Hyundai, but the difference can, without question, be explained and understood by anyone—including you!

ART AS AN INVESTMENT

Buy art because you like it, not for investment reasons. *Again: Never buy art purely for investment.* Artists do not sit in their studios deliberating about how to create commodities that will compete well with stocks, bonds, oil futures, or other artists' art. Monet did not wonder, for example, about how his Giverny canvases would perform financially over time or how they would compete against works of the Munich School. Don't insult artists or art dealers and trivialize their art by viewing it as currency.

Far too many buyers are attracted to art because they have either heard, read, or otherwise become aware that certain works of art have substantially increased in value over time. They don't know much about art, but they do know that they would like to make some money by owning it. The most unfortunate of these speculators end up paying highly inflated prices to charlatan dealers who talk only money and speak of art as the path to riches.

We are all aware that some art does increase in value over time and that many art experts and advanced collectors consider the financial consequences of their purchases. But if you ask these people what attracts them to art above all else, money is always far down the list. If you also ask these people what percentage of art increases in value over time, their unanimous answer will be, "Not very much." The great majority of art produced on this planet fades slowly into obscurity. You'll have a much easier time, for example, finding a $2,000 work of art that will be worth $500 in ten years than finding a $2,000 work of art that will be worth $4,000 after that same amount of time.

Without exception, reputable dealers agree that if what you buy happens to go up in value, that's great and you're fortunate. If it doesn't, that's fine, too, because it will continue to beautify your environment and provide you with pleasure for as long as you own it.

WHY SOME ART INCREASES IN VALUE

Only the very best art is destined for fame, fortune, and financial stardom. When you read in the newspapers or hear on the news, for example, that "art" has increased in value by a certain amount per year over the past so many years, know that masterworks by the world's great artists are what they are referring to. They do not mean every piece of art that has ever been produced.

Art that increases in value does so because acknowledged art experts such as museum curators, established art dealers, and art scholars view it as significant in some way and agree that it should be recognized, honored, or distinguished above all other art. For example, when a major museum decides to put on a one-person show of a particular artist's work, anything that artist has done in the past or will produce in the future tends to increase in value. The museum show focuses attention on the artist, legitimizes the art in the eyes of the art-buying community, attracts new collectors, and, in general, increases demand for that artist's work. Art that is "worth more" in the opinion of the experts also tends to be worth more in dollars and cents.

A distinction must be made here between real and artificial increases in value. Real increases, as stated above, have to do with general consensus among experts in the art community that certain art has merit above other art. Artificial increases have to do with art galleries arbitrarily raising their asking prices either for no apparent reason or for reasons they concoct on their own.

For example, suppose you walk into Triple-A Fine Arts Gallery and see a limited edition print. The asking price is $3,500. The gallery owner tells you that only last year the print could be purchased for $1,750. When the edition sells out, she adds, the price will go even higher. Assume that this is an artificial price increase if the artist has not accomplished anything significant over the past year, if no experts have recently commended the artist for outstanding achievements, and if no outside evidence can be presented to justify the increase. Assume that the gallery owner has simply decided to increase her profit margin.

Sooner or later, art that has been artificially inflated in price deflates back down to "reality," while art that legitimately increases in value usually maintains its value or continues to increase in value. Time and continual assessment by art experts, not hype or declaration, determine what is great in art, what increases in value, and what should be forever forgotten.

A LOOK AHEAD

With these basic art and money facts in mind, let's move on to the specifics— namely, evaluating the asking prices of whatever works of art you have selected for possible purchase. Being able to understand a given work of art in terms of a set dollar value is the final goal of buying art smart. How much art are you getting for how much money? That's the question you will learn how to answer in the following chapter.

CHAPTER 16

How to Evaluate Art Prices

Any work of art you see for sale and are interested in owning has a price attached to it. If you're like most collectors, you want to make sure that price is fair and reasonable before you pay it. You make that determination by evaluating that price.

You may wonder how you can possibly determine on your own whether or not art asking prices are fair, but it's really not that difficult once you know how. In fact, evaluating art prices is much like evaluating the price of any consumer product you are considering buying: you find out what you want to know from the firm representing the product, and then you check independently to make sure that what they tell you is true.

Unfortunately, not all art dealers appreciate collectors who know how to evaluate prices. They resent buyers who ask too many questions, and they would rather sell to clients who believe that dollar values are set according to mystical procedures that only art dealers can understand. Know right now that that's simply not the case!

The single most important truth about art prices is that they are deliberately set according to methods that you or anyone else can understand, and, furthermore, they may be verified as reasonable or unreasonable just as deliberately. You need a certain amount of knowledge to reach those conclusions, of course, but once you've acquired it, you'll be capable of making them entirely on your own. Never allow anyone to convince you otherwise.

Before going any further, be advised that the procedures outlined here for evaluating art prices are not meant to take the place of the art research described in Part III of this book. Buying art based on financial considerations alone, without any understanding of the artists, the art, or the history behind the art, comes under the category of pure speculation and is an extremely high-risk proposition. You cannot intelligently evaluate an asking price without doing your research first.

Many novice art buyers don't fully understand what price evaluation entails. They ask what few price questions they have to ask at the galleries selling the art, blindly accept everything they are told, and assume that no further investigation is necessary. They believe that they achieve adequate insight into asking prices when in fact they accomplish nothing of the sort. Galleries are, of course, more than happy to answer money questions about their art, but in the great majority of cases, you have an obvious conflict of interest.

What gallery do you know that believes its asking prices are anything but fair? What gallery do you know that will advise you not to buy its art because it is overpriced? The answer to both questions is *none*. Buyers don't necessarily get taken advantage of when their entire price evaluation consists of asking sellers price questions, but at the very best they get biased opinions.

Comprehensive art price evaluation means more than having a quick chat with the seller. You've got to accumulate a variety of data from throughout the art community in order to get a balanced overview of the value of any art you are considering buying. You acquire this data from three primary sources:

- *The seller.* When evaluating asking prices, acquiring information from the sellers is the only sensible way to start. They are experts at what they sell and can provide extensive data about asking prices.

- *Art auctions.* By studying price results of art that has sold at auction—specifically, art that is comparable to what you are considering buying—you can get an idea of what your art would be worth outside of its gallery setting and of the overall strength of the market for that art.

- *Resources that do not have a conflict of interests.* By consulting independent art experts who have no vested interest in whatever art you are considering buying, you can get informed, unbiased opinions on the prices you are being asked to pay.

This check and balance system protects you from overpaying for art. Learn how to use it and profit.

ASKING THE SELLER

As mentioned above, art price research always begins with the seller. The single most important and only absolutely necessary question to ask any seller, no matter what you are being offered, is this: *"How did you arrive at your asking price?"*

A satisfactory answer—that is, the type of answer you want—is one that explains and justifies the price you are being asked to pay in terms of specific current market information about the art and its artist. Without exception, a satisfactory answer must include concrete data about other works of art by that artist that have already been sold, the circumstances under which they have sold, and how much they have sold for.

You want facts here, actual sales results—persons, places, dates, dollar amounts—and the more you get, the better. You want proof that work by the artist is changing hands on a regular basis at prices comparable to those that you are being asked to pay. And you want information about who is selling it *besides* the gallery that is offering you the art—auction houses, other art galleries, and so on. When you get these sorts of detailed responses to that most important price question, you know you're dealing with reputable dealers.

An unsatisfactory answer to the big question—an answer that may appear to justify an asking price, but actually does not—is when sellers tell you that other dealers' asking prices are comparable to what you are being asked to pay. This information gets you nowhere. Asking price alone is never an indication of market strength or fair market value, and the asking price is irrelevant until someone actually pays it. To repeat: *The amount of money a work of art is being offered for by an art gallery is not necessarily how much that art is worth.* It's nothing more than how much the gallery hopes to sell it for.

Another unsatisfactory answer is one that only relates price information about sales that have been made at the gallery trying to sell you the art. Price records solely from the seller's gallery are never adequate proof that what you are being asked to pay is fair or that a market exists for the art outside of that gallery's doors. Even when a gallery has sold numerous works of art at prices comparable to what you are being asked to pay, this could mean nothing more than that the gallery personnel are experts at talking people into buying that art or that they sell primarily to clients who neglect to evaluate the prices of what they buy before they buy it. You need additional information about what is happening in other segments of the market.

Whatever answer you get to the big question, record every single detail of it. You are then ready to continue your price evaluation outside of the gallery selling the art and see what the rest of the art community has to say.

CHECKING ART AUCTION PRICES

The amount of money a work of art sells for at auction is an excellent indicator of how liquid that art is, how strong its market is, and what it is worth when it has to sell immediately for cash. High auction prices indicate that a healthy, no-hype market exists for an artist. Low auction prices, on the other hand, indicate a weak or unstable market. It's that simple.

A major goal of your price evaluation is to approximate how much any work of art you are interested in buying would sell for at auction and then to compare that value to the price you are being asked to pay. You need to make this comparison not because you intend to sell the art but because, as a person who buys art smart, you want it to have some degree of financial strength on the open market, outside of its biased retail environment and in the neutral auction setting. In other words, you don't want it to be worthless the moment you walk it out the gallery door.

Art auctions take place continually around the world. Tens of thousands of works of art are auctioned annually. Auction houses sell everything from Old Masters to contemporary art, and an average sale consists of between 100 and 300 pieces. All major auction houses and a number of less important ones publish catalogues of every art sale they conduct.

Learning how to read auction catalogues is an essential part of art price evaluation. These publications are the most important source of art price information in the art business. A single catalogue can supply you with comprehensive price data on several hundred works of art.

Almost all art dealers have auction catalogues in their libraries and will be happy to teach you how to read them. A few minutes is all it takes. For our purposes now, what you need to know is explained below.

Auction catalogues individually list each work of art to be sold along with basic facts about it. An average catalogue listing for a work of art includes the lot number of the art in the sale; the name and nationality of the artist; the artist's birth (and death) date; the title, medium, and dimensions of the art; the location and spelling of the signature as it appears on the art; and the estimated amount of money the auction house thinks the piece will sell for. Entries also note whether the art is illustrated in the catalogue. (The better houses illustrate many of the works of art that they sell, sometimes in color, but mostly in black and white.)

Let's imagine you are studying an auction catalogue listing on a painting by an artist named Blake Stoneman and that it provides the following information:

Lot Number: 4027
Artist: Blake Stoneman; American (1912–1981)
Title: Northern Coast on a Stormy Day
Signature and location: "B. Stoneman" in the lower left corner
Medium: Oil on canvas
Dimensions: 27 by 36 inches (68.5 by 91.5 centimeters)

Estimated selling price: $1,000–$2,000
Illustrated in the catalogue

No matter what auction house is selling this picture, the actual catalogue entry would look something like this:

*4027   Blake Stoneman (1912–1981)

Northern Coast on a Stormy Day

Signed lower left: B. Stoneman
Oil on canvas   27 by 36 inches
                                           68.5 by 91.5 cm

See illustration   (Est: 1,000/2,000)

After an auction sale is held, all prices realized at that sale become a matter of public record. Anyone can contact the auction house to find out how much any item in that particular sale sold for. Let's say that the Blake Stoneman painting sells for $2,500. You can call the auction house and ask how much it sold for (this amount is known as the *auction record* for that painting) and also ask for auction records of other Stoneman paintings the auction house has handled in the past. The auction house will give you those results.

Suppose you are interested in finding out how much Blake Stoneman paintings have been selling for at auction houses around the world. This would involve contacting auction house after auction house to see whether they have ever sold his art and, if so, how much it sold for. You can see that this would be an extremely difficult, expensive, and time-consuming task. To make matters worse, auction houses are not generally enthusiastic about giving out price information to people evaluating art asking prices.

Fortunately, you don't have to bother auction houses with continual price requests. You or anyone else can locate all the auction records you want simply and easily because several publishers keep track of auction sales in books known as *auction record compendiums*. These references are published annually and each volume includes one year's worth—tens of thousands—of auction records from numerous auction houses throughout the world. See Appendix 2 for a list of the major auction record compendiums and brief comments on their respective strong points.

These volumes sell for between $85 and $300 each, but you don't need to buy them to use them. Most major public library, museum, college, and university art departments have auction records in their art reference sections. Find out which libraries carry which auction records, and when you need information, just call or visit these institutions and ask the art librarians to supply you with whatever auction records you need.

Make sure you have access to most and preferably all major compendiums, because they often differ in the quality and amount of information they provide. Not every library has them all, and some libraries carry only one or two. If you have to contact more than one library in order to cover all auction records, do so. Art dealers and serious collectors generally have auction records in their galleries, too, but most are reluctant to share them with you unless they know you well.

Auction records are easy to read and understand. Each compendium has instructions on how to read results, and all compendiums list results in basically the same format. Artists are listed alphabetically, and individual price results on any particular artist are listed from highest to lowest dollar amounts. Under Blake Stoneman, for example, you would find the $2,500 entry and entries for other Stoneman paintings that sold during that year.

The $2,500 Stoneman entry would look something like this in an auction compendium:

Stoneman, Blake   American (1912–1981)

$2,500   Northern Coast on a Stormy Day, signed lower
              left (10/12/89, Smith's-NY, #4027, illus.), 27 by 36
              inches, oil on canvas.

This entry gives the same basic information about Stoneman and his painting that you find in the auction house's sale catalogue. Inside the second set of parentheses are the date of the sale (10/12/89), the name of the auction house (Smith's), the location of the auction house (New York), the lot number of the painting, and the notation that the painting is illustrated in Smith's catalogue of that sale. Note that auction compendiums do not illustrate paintings the way auction catalogues do. If you need to know what particular works of art look like, you must refer to the actual sales catalogues.

APPROXIMATING A WORK'S AUCTION VALUE

Suppose you have selected a work of art for possible purchase, have reached the point in your research where you are seriously considering buying it, and now wish to determine its approximate auction value. The procedure is the same no matter what type of art or artist you are evaluating, but for our purposes here, let's say you are considering a Blake Stoneman mountain scene, 24 by 30 inches, with an asking price of $4,500.

Your first step is to locate as many auction records as possible of Stoneman paintings that have sold at auction in recent years. Here's how you do this for any artist:

- *Personally check or have art librarians check auction compendiums for price results.* Ask art librarians, experienced collectors, or other experts to work with you until you know what you're doing, and remember to check all the different compendiums, not just one or two.

- *Start with the most recent year's auction results and locate all entries under the artist's name.* Repeat the procedure going back through at least three years' worth of compendiums (you should preferably check five to ten years' worth).

- *Write down or copy full listings of all pieces of the artist's work that have sold during the time period you are checking.*

- *Whenever possible, check actual auction catalogues when compendiums note that items are illustrated.* You need to compare as many pieces as possible to the one whose value you are in the process of approximating. Obtaining specific catalogues usually involves contacting the individual auction houses (unless you happen to be on friendly terms with dealers or collectors who have the catalogues in their libraries).

You are now ready to take the auction records you have located and approximate an auction value for your Stoneman painting or whatever art you are evaluating. Below are set forth some general rules that will help you analyze, interpret, and understand those records and apply them to your art.

The Most Significant Auction Records for Your Purposes Are Those That Describe Works of Art Most Similar In Size, Subject Matter, Medium, Date Executed, and Other Particulars to the One You Are Researching. The amounts of money these works sell for are the best approximations of your art's auction value. In our Blake Stoneman example, since you are researching an oil painting of a mountain scene measuring 24 by 30 inches, you would pay special attention to auction records of mountain scene oil paintings with similar qualifications. You would not dwell on records of a painting of ships on the ocean that measured 6 by 9 inches, a floral still-life watercolor, and so on. Comparing the selling prices for the ship scene or the still life to your mountain scene would be like comparing apples and oranges.

Auction Prices of Art Similar to the Art You Are Evaluating Should Generally Be at Least 40 to 50 Percent of What the Gallery Is Asking You to Pay. You do not, for example, want to pay a gallery $4,500 for the Stoneman painting you are considering when similar paintings sell at auction for only $300 to $500 each. Remember that auction prices are an excellent indicator of value on the open market and that, in the great majority of cases, records that are consistently far below gallery retail indicate a weak or unstable market for that art.

The Works of Art That Sell for the Greatest Amounts of Money Are Usually the Ones That Collectors of That Artist Prize the Most. If, for example, Stoneman mountain scenes bring the highest prices at auction, assume that they are more sought-after by collectors than are any other subject matters. The more characteristics a work of art you are researching has of the higher-priced works of a particular artist, the more you should think about buying it.

The Works of Art That Sell for the Least Amounts of Money Are Usually the Least Desirable in Terms of Collectibility. If Stoneman mountain scenes sell for less than all other subject matters do, assume they are not in demand by collectors. When art you are researching falls into the low end of the artist's auction price continuum, think about looking for something a little more collectible.

Pay the Most Attention to Those Dollar Amounts That the Majority of the Art in Question Auctions for, Not the Minority. For example, if you locate twenty different auction records for Stoneman paintings, nineteen of which are in the $2,000-to-$3,000 price range and one for $15,000, assume that Stoneman pieces auction in the low thousands of dollars, not the tens of thousands. Isolated high (or low) price records are not accurate market indicators.

See How Auction Prices Change Over Time. You want indications that an artist's art is at least holding steady and preferably increasing in value. Watch out when you see decreasing or erratic records.

You Need at Least Half a Dozen Auction Records to Establish Any Pattern for an Artist. One or two isolated records of pieces selling at auction cannot be relied upon to provide any concrete conclusions about a particular artist's market. What you can conclude from one or two auction records, though, is that the artist has at least been through auction and is at least viewed by auction galleries as salable in a public arena. In other words, the existence of any auction records is better than no records at all.

Let's return now to our Blake Stoneman mountain scene and analyze it in terms of some hypothetical auction records. Suppose you locate ten auction records of Stoneman oil paintings that have sold over the past five years, with characteristics as follows:

• The selling prices range from a low of $300 to a high of $4,000.

• Two are mountain scenes, five are coastal scenes, and three are land-scapes.

• One mountain scene is about the same size as the painting you like; the other is much smaller. They sold for $2,000 and $350 respectively. The $2,000 painting sold four years ago.

• The three highest records—$4,000, $3,500, and $3,000—are all coastal scenes and all about the same size as your mountain scene.

• The remaining records are for landscapes, the smallest selling for $300, the largest for $900.

• In general, Stoneman's prices have been slowly increasing over the past five years.

Based on this data, you can make certain assumptions about Stoneman's market, determine an approximate auction value for your mountain scene painting, and compare it to the gallery's $4,500 asking price. The following interpretations and conclusions would be considered reasonable by the great majority of art experts:

• Stoneman collectors prefer coastal scenes over mountain scenes and land-scapes (his three highest auction records are all coastal scenes).

• Mountain scenes are acceptable to collectors as evidenced by the fact that the larger one fetched a respectable price.

• Stoneman's landscapes are not very collectible; they all sold low.

• Collectors prefer larger paintings over small ones; the small ones sell cheaply.

• The auction value of the mountain scene you are thinking about buying would probably be between $2,000 and $2,500. This price estimate is based on the similarity in size and composition of yours to the mountain scene that sold for $2,000. The $2,500 high estimate takes into consideration the fact that the $2,000 record is four years old and that the Stoneman market is stable and gradually strengthening.

• Comparing that $2,000 to $2,500 auction approximation to the $4,500 asking price, you could conclude that $4,500 is, at worst, just slightly on the high side, but not overly so. You could call it fair retail because even the lower auction value of $2,000 falls within 40 to 50 percent of the gallery retail.

Suppose you are evaluating an asking price and find only a few low auction records for the artist or, worse yet, none at all? This is not usually a good sign. In most cases, this means that the artist's market is weak; the auctions are not interested in handling his or her work because it won't sell for very much money. Exceptions do exist, though. For instance, an artist might be so collectible or rare that collectors hold on to their art and rarely resell it. Art research, as well as conversations with the seller and with no-conflict resources, usually indicates whether this is the case or not, but nevertheless, you're still in the dark as to performance at auction.

No matter what the reason for a lack of auction data, you are by no means at a dead end. You can still approximate an auction value on the art. It's a little different from the normal procedure, but not very difficult.

To get the approximate auction value in such a case, contact at least several auction houses, both regional and national, that conduct regular art sales. (See Appendix 3 for a list of significant American auction houses.) Speak with art experts on their staffs. Ask every specialist you speak with the following two questions:

1. Are you familiar with this artist?

2. Would you auction his or her work if given the opportunity?

It's good when the auction experts answer yes to both parts of this inquiry, not so good when they say yes to the first and no to the second, and worse yet when they say no to both.

Whenever someone at an auction house gives you at least one yes answer, ask whether that person can give you ballpark estimates of what art similar to the art you are considering buying might sell for at one of the auction's sales. Don't automatically assume that the values you get are the approximate amounts that the art would actually auction for. These dollar figures do come from informed sources, though, and should be given serious consideration. This is especially true when every firm you call gives you the same approximate values. Regardless of the responses you get, always combine them with seller and no-conflict-resource inquiries.

As an aside, don't get into the habit of constantly calling auction houses for this sort of advice, especially when you can locate adequate price information elsewhere. Auction firms are in the business of selling art, not running price information hotlines.

CONSULTING NO-CONFLICT-OF-INTEREST RESOURCES

The consultation of no-conflict-of-interest resources is equally as important as auction price evaluation and is the other procedure you must employ in order to corroborate any price information sellers give you. In such consultations you solicit the thoughts, feedback, and prognostications of the experts regarding your selections. This information, combined with auction price evaluation and with what the seller tells you, is, in the great majority of cases, all you need to determine the fairness of an asking price.

No-conflict research becomes all the more important when few or no auction records exist for an artist whose art you are considering. In these cases, no-conflict resources provide the only conclusive price information you have to go on outside of what a seller tells you.

No-conflict-of-interest resources are exactly what they sound like—they are dealers, collectors, and other experts who are independent from and have no vested interest whatsoever in the art or artist you are researching or the gallery you are patronizing. Ideally, they do not sell or collect that art on a regular basis, and profits from any related transactions they may be involved in do not constitute a significant portion of their incomes. Above all, these resources should be individuals you know and trust.

A no-conflict resource can be anyone you meet in the course of your art-buying activities. Over time, you get to know certain authorities who eventually become friends or acquaintances you can confide in about your collecting. The better you know each other, the more such a person is willing to help you by giving you honest advice whenever you need it.

For example, an art dealer you have never done business with before is not likely to comment on a work of art you are considering buying that hangs in another dealer's gallery. To her you are a stranger asking pointed questions that could involve her taking sides or incriminating the other dealer. But the better she gets to know you and to understand your intentions, the more likely she'll be to give you the valued opinion you want.

Be patient about acquiring no-conflict resources. You'll eventually fig-

151

ure out which individuals you work best with and are able to trust as honest, unbiased resources for consistent and accurate price information.

Here are the types of questions you should ask your no-conflict resources about a piece of art you are considering buying:

- *Have you ever heard of this artist?* The more recognizable the artist's name, the better. No name recognition, on the other hand, is never a good sign. Combined with poor or nonexistent auction records, this could mean that you stop here, forget about the artist, and look for something else to buy. Assuming you get at least some name recognition, proceed with your questions.

- *What do you think about the artist's art and progress as an artist?* You want to hear that no-conflict resources respect the work of the artist and have good things to say about his or her future.

- *What do you think about the market for this artist's work?* In responses to this question you want indications that the market is broad-based and increasing. The greater the variety of galleries, experts, and collectors supporting an artist's work, financially as well as critically, the better. Look for signs that prices the art sells for are at least holding steady, and preferably increasing.

- *This question is for no-conflict dealers only: Would you handle this artist's work if someone offered it to you for sale, and, if so, how much would you charge for it?* This is an important question. The more galleries that answer yes and the closer their hypothetical selling prices are to what you are being asked to pay, the better. Also, the more enthusiastic no-conflict galleries are about handling the art, the better.

- *Again, for dealers only: If you are willing to sell this artist's art, how fast do you think you can sell it?* The faster, the better. An estimated selling time of a month or less is a sign of an active market and a desirable artist. A year is not. In fact, galleries who think a year or more is necessary to sell the art would most likely not be willing to sell it in the first place.

- *For no-conflict collectors and other experts who do not buy and sell art for a living: Do you already own work by this artist, or, if you don't, would you consider buying a piece for your collection?* You want *yes* answers; you want enthusiastic answers.

- *Here's what the art I'm thinking about buying looks like, and here's how much I'm being asked to pay for it. What do you think?* This is the most important question because the more no-conflict resources who view your situation as acceptable, the more you should consider buying the art. It's also the most difficult question because anyone who answers it is required to take a position on another dealer and his or her art. Since it is so direct, ask it only to those no-conflict resources whom you confide in the most. Seriously consider all answers you get here in making your final decision.

Get to know as many no-conflict resources as possible who are qualified to answer your financial—as well as aesthetic and informational—questions about art. The greater number of these individuals you know and consult, the more data you can acquire and the better informed a decision you can make regarding whatever art you have selected. Remember to cultivate these relationships gradually and diplomatically so that you can ask sensitive questions like the last one and get truthful, helpful answers.

By the way, you don't need 100 percent enthusiasm and perfect positive answers to every question from every authority you consult. A variety of responses is fine. What you should look for, though, is an overall positive response to the art and artist in question.

In summation, when no-conflict resources recognize the name of your artist, you're off to a good start. When they say positive things about the artist, that's better. When they express a willingness to actually tie up gallery space and sell the art or display it in their collections, that's best. When they comment favorably on the asking price of the particular piece you are thinking about buying, that's about all you need to go ahead and buy.

One final note. Just because an asking price turns out to be too high or an artist turns out to be not that well known throughout the art community, do not automatically refuse to buy the art. If you really love it, go ahead and buy it, no matter what it is. *You can buy any art at any time at any price and for whatever reason.* All that price evaluation techniques provide you with is a knowledge of the dollars and cents aspects of that art.

USING ART PRICE GUIDES AS RESEARCH TOOLS

Art price guides do exist, and they are fast becoming popular with collectors as "quick fix" references for evaluating asking prices. They are very affordable—most cost less than $30 each—as well as easy to get a hold of and easy to use. However, they also have severe limitations as reference tools, limitations you should be aware of so that you don't place to much emphasis on the information they provide.

Price guides are designed to give brief biographical information about artists in combination with either several sample auction records or low-to-high price ranges. Price data they provide comes almost exclusively from auction records. A typical price guide listing would look something like this:

Stoneman, Blake; American (1912–1981) paintings: $300–4,000

This listing gives you the artist's name, nationality, and birth and death dates, and it also tells you that his paintings sell at auction for between $300 and $4,000.

Let's say you're researching that 24- by 30-inch Blake Stoneman mountain scene from our earlier example by consulting a price guide as opposed to auction records. All you can tell from this price guide listing is that Stoneman paintings have been through auction and have auctioned in the $300-to-$4,000 range. That's it.

Here's what you cannot tell:

- You cannot tell how many auction sales that price range is based on—it may be two, or it may be fifty.

- You cannot tell what type of paintings sell in the $4,000 range and what type sell in the $300 range.

- You cannot tell what subject matters bring the best prices, the worst prices, and average prices.

- You cannot tell what sizes bring the best and worst prices.

- You cannot tell how price results are grouped. For example, twenty Stoneman paintings may have auctioned for $300–$500 and only one for $4,000.

The bottom line is this: Use art price guides with extreme caution, and never make a decision about whether or not to buy a work of art based only on entries in price guides. Price guides are good to check when you need quick, general price information, but that's as far as you should go with them. Note whatever price information you find, but always check auction records and no-conflict resources for the full story on exactly what has sold for how much.

Appendix 2 contains a list of the most popular price guides and comments about each. If you happen to be researching an artist in price guides, check that artist's entry in every guide you can. As with auction record compendiums, information often varies from one guide to the next.

A LOOK AHEAD

At this point, you should have no trouble deciding how fair or reasonable an asking price is. In other words, you're finally done with all your research and evaluations! Can you believe it? You're ready to buy art.

But wait one last minute. Suppose you could buy that art for less than the seller is asking for it? If you find this possibility appealing, then the next chapter is for you.

CHAPTER 17

Negotiating a Purchase

You're ready to write out your check and buy a piece of art except for one small detail: you'd like to pay less for it. Whether you think the price is too high, you have a policy never to pay full retail, or you love to bargain, you're not quite ready to complete the transaction. So where do you stand?

You happen to be in luck. Art dealers have been known to leave room in their asking prices for negotiation or, as it is more commonly called, bargaining. You may just get a break on the money issue if you know how to conduct yourself.

Reasons for flexibility in asking prices vary. Dealers know that certain clients expect "deals" or that they enjoy bargaining; galleries leave room for employee commissions; outside market factors sometimes force dealers to pad asking prices; dealers themselves may accept or in rare instances encourage bargaining as part of the art-buying process; and so on. Whatever the situation, art buyers and sellers negotiate final selling prices all the time.

In its most primitive form, bargaining consists of two opposing parties battling against each other for no reason other than money. The seller wants to sell for as much as possible, and the buyer wants to pay as little as possible. Anything goes, and the one who outsmarts the other with the cleverest tactics wins.

Mature bargaining or negotiating, on the other hand, is far from a simple battle over who can make who pay the most or sell for the least amount of money. Good bargaining is a cooperative venture in which both buyer and seller sit down together with the intention of reaching an agreement on how much a particular work of art is worth. Research results are studied, price data is evaluated, arguments from both sides are considered, and value is determined to the satisfaction of both parties. When agreement is reached, the art sells.

Negotiating art prices is not a sport. It is a tool for addressing a situation in which you believe that an asking price is too high. In such a situation, rather than throwing up your hands and walking out the gallery door, speak with the seller about what you think that price should be. Make an offer. Consider bargaining as a petitionary process through which you request that the person in a position of power (the seller) reconsider his or her decision to price the art at the level he or she has.

Intelligent bargaining or negotiating begins by your presenting a well-constructed and well-documented case about what you think a particular selling price should be and why. The seller, in turn, either accepts that offer, makes a counteroffer, or states that the asking price is firm and refuses to consider any offer. You then respond to the seller, and so the process continues until the two of you either agree or else agree to disagree.

The procedure may sound easy, but negotiating for art is an art in itself. You can do it right, and you can do it wrong. Learn the fine points and etiquette of bargaining in order to get what you want and get it without offending anyone the next time you think you should be paying less than what you are being asked to pay.

HOW A NEGOTIATING RELATIONSHIP EVOLVES

When you are about to buy art from a gallery for the first time, you have no idea how the owner feels about bargaining, and the owner has no idea how you feel about his or her asking prices. The moment you begin to find these things out about each other is the moment you decide to negotiate an asking price. At that point, opinions about how high or low prices are begin to emerge from both sides.

This first encounter over money is a difficult time in any dealer–collector relationship. At the very least, you have to be diplomatic and sensitive to the seller's feelings. You can easily offend by making an offer, because you are essentially saying that you think the art is worth less than the dealer thinks it's worth. Make mistakes at the outset, and you can seriously damage or even destroy a relationship before it really begins. Make an intelligent offer, though, and you'll find that the seller will listen to and respect what you have to say.

The outcome of a first negotiation affects you in two ways. The obvious one is that a particular asking price is evaluated and agreed upon to the apparent satisfaction of both you and the seller. The not-so-obvious outcome—but much more far-reaching one—is that the two of you begin to discover each other's positions on how art transactions should progress to completion. You set the tone for all future dealings with that seller.

During the next few negotiations, you pretty much determine the course of your business relationship together. Consistent positive outcomes mean that you each come closer and closer to understanding what the other wants, and, as a result, every successive negotiation becomes easier than the last.

The seller develops a good idea of the most you are willing to pay and you get a feel for the least he or she is willing to accept.

The twofold object of successful negotiating is, therefore, to buy art at prices you want to pay and, at the same time, to keep sellers working for you, keep them on your side. Poor bargaining technique may net you a good price on one or two pieces of artwork in the short run, but in the long run, your collecting suffers because dealers get put off by your bad buying habits. Knowing how to negotiate means knowing how to buy art smart.

PROPER BARGAINING ETIQUETTE: DOS AND DON'TS

The first and most important step toward intelligent negotiating is knowing when *not* to negotiate. *When you see art you like and you determine through research that the asking price is fair, buy it without making an offer.* Intelligent collectors respect sellers' abilities to price art accurately and always recognize when those prices are fair to begin with. Sellers, in return, treat those collectors with equivalent respect.

When You Honestly Believe an Asking Price Is Too High, Do Make an Offer. Before you present that offer, though, research and organize evidence to back it up. Take time to build your case. Make sure you can give a solid presentation and support everything you say with facts. Dealers do not appreciate frivolous offers and can quickly tell whether you have a legitimate concern or are just trying to pay less for the sake of paying less.

Do Make Your Offers Reasonable Ones That Dealers Can Conceivably Accept. Extremely low offers lead to bad feelings much more often than they lead to completed sales. Dealers can only reduce prices so far before they are taking losses on their art, and no dealer is interested in doing that. When the offer you want to make is far below the asking price, think seriously about not making it and buying something else instead. Dealers never appreciate "lowball" offers.

Do Be Tactful, and Pay Close Attention to Sellers' Reactions as You Go. Sellers should be receptive to what you say at all stages of the negotiations. They love having intelligent discussions about art, even when the end result might mean that they may have to lower their prices. Know when to stop, though, once the dealer begins to lose interest in what you have to say. With experience, you'll be able to tell exactly when that is.

Do Base Offers on Facts About the Art, Not Facts About Your Personal Financial Situation. For example, suppose you see a sculpture you like and determine that the $1,000 asking price is fair. If your budget is only $500 per work of art, don't arbitrarily offer the dealer $500 for the sculpture. Either wait until you can afford to buy it, or shop instead for sculptures more in your price range.

Do Learn How Individual Dealers React to Your Offers. You will find that every dealer has his or her own peculiarities in bargaining situations. Knowing what those quirks are helps to reduce friction during negotiations. There is no universally "right" way to negotiate, and it helps to tailor your bargaining techniques somewhat for each of the dealers you negotiate with.

Do Make an Offer Only After the Seller Has Had the Art for a While and Has Not Been Able to Sell It. A month is a good minimum waiting time. If you're not sure how long the art has been for sale, ask. If you make an offer on a fresh new arrival before the dealer has a chance to show it to other potential buyers, that dealer will almost certainly take offense.

Do Pay Close Attention to Dealers' Overall Responses to Your Offers. The best dealers give you positive, constructive responses during negotiations that teach you about art and the art business. Whether or not they accept the offers, they supply you with important information about why they feel their asking prices are fair and how they set them, and thus they continue to educate you at all times. Avoid dealers who are not interested in having price-related discussions or who consistently refuse your offers without giving any reasons why.

Knowing what *not* to do in a negotiating situation is just as important as knowing what *to* do. You make offers in hopes that they will be accepted, so you certainly don't want to sabotage yourself during the bargaining process. Avoid certain behaviors and you'll maximize the chances of getting what you want.

The Most Important Don't Is This: Don't Start Talking Price the Moment You See Something You Like. This is not only rude, but it also alienates sellers. You give them the impression that all you care about is money and that you're inclined to give as little of it away as possible. Even when you know precisely what you want to offer the moment you see a piece of art and can back that offer with facts, get to know the seller before diving right in and making your offer.

Don't Make an Offer Without Carefully Thinking It Through, because the Seller Just Might Surprise You and Accept It. When a seller accepts your offer, you are obliged to buy the art. Dealers do not appreciate collectors who make offers, have them accepted, and then decide that they are not interested in buying the art after all. This is bad etiquette and will seriously impair future negotiations.

When No Price Tag Is Visible On a Piece of Art and You Have to Ask How Much It Costs, Don't Give the Impression That You Think It's Too High the Moment You Hear It. Avoid rolling your eyes, groaning, making faces, and that sort of thing. Dealers dislike collectors who have knee-jerk reactions to selling prices.

Don't Negotiate for the Sport of it or Suggest That an Asking Price Is Too High on Art That You're Not Really Interested In Buying. Make offers only when you're serious.

Don't Get a Reputation as Someone Who Always Wants Everything for Less, Someone Who Thinks That the Asking Price is Always Too High, No Matter What It Is. Dealers will stop showing you good salable art and show you only second-rate or hard-to-sell pieces that they don't mind getting rid of at bargain prices—and that's assuming they'll want you around their galleries in the first place.

Don't Bargain When You're Shown Special Consideration. For example, when a dealer calls you first to see a piece of art that has just arrived, either buy it or pass on it. Do not bargain. The dealer is showing you special treatment, and you should return the favor. If you think the price is too high, wait until the dealer has had the art for a while, had a chance to show it to other collectors, and has not been able to sell it. Then make your offer.

Don't Talk About All the Great Art Bargains You've Gotten in the Past While in the Process of Negotiating a Price. Not only is this irritating, but it also gives the seller the idea that you only buy art when it's cheap. Why should a dealer bother showing you anything if all you talk about is how little you paid for something similar two years ago or how a dealer across town once sold you a such-and-such for half what it was worth?

Don't Beat a Seller Over the Head With an Offer. When a dealer tells you he or she would rather not sell at the price you want to pay, don't continue to give reasons why you should get it for less. Even if the seller does eventually give in, you'll pay for those few saved dollars in future negotiations.

ADVANCED NEGOTIATING

Gain experience negotiating with dealers by keeping your offers conservative at first and making them only when you feel absolutely justified in doing so.

As with any learned and practiced skill, the more offers you make, the better you get at making them. After awhile, you'll acquire a feel for how far you can go in any given situation, even with dealers you've never met before. You'll not only know more about the art you collect and what it's worth on the open market, but you'll also know more about how to bargain for it.

Expert bargainers can closely approximate how much dealers they've never met before are willing to accept for their art even before negotiations begin. They recognize differences between sellers who are firm on their asking prices and those who are flexible. They know just the right moments to offer just the right amounts. Offers are still based in fact and reason, but in advanced negotiating a little more strategy comes into play in terms of timing, the way the offer is proposed, and so on.

The ideal situation for you or any buyer is to determine the least amount of money a dealer is willing to accept for an artwork without being offended or insulted. The fact is that in any negotiating situation, this "least amount" does exist. The more money you can save without damaging a relationship, the more money you'll have to spend on future acquisitions. Being able to determine "least amounts" is not really a skill you can learn through study, so don't start signing up for "How to Get What You Want" seminars or run to the library and read all the books you can on negotiating technique. You learn only through experience.

Another point that advanced negotiators are aware of and take into consideration is that art prices often fluctuate according to sellers' moods, financial situations, frequency of recent sales, feelings about particular works of art, and so on. For example, a dealer who hasn't made a sale in several weeks and needs to pay bills is more willing to consider offers than one who is making regular sales.

Some dealers are more inclined to entertain offers at certain times of the year than at others. For example, the summer months are often slow months for art galleries and, therefore, good times for making offers. On the flip side, fall is a busy time of year, a time when your offers are less likely to be accepted.

In many instances, the longer a dealer has had a work of art in stock, the more open he or she will be to taking offers on it. Sooner or later, a dealer may get tired of looking at the same old art, may decide to increase available storage space, and so on.

With time, you'll be able to take greater risks when the moment of monetary truth is at hand. For now, be conservative and don't take too many chances too fast. You want negotiations to be cooperative ventures, not combative ones.

Surprisingly, the most advanced and mature form of negotiating is no negotiating at all. In such situations, you and a seller understand each other so well that selling prices are agreed upon instantly. This goal of complete understanding and total trust is one you should strive for. In the end, the less time you waste bargaining, the more time you can devote to collecting.

A LOOK AHEAD

So let's say you make an offer on a work of art, and the seller accepts it. The big moment has arrived. You take out your checkbook and get ready to write. Time to buy!

Or is it?

Buying art is a little more complicated than simply writing a check and walking out the gallery door with your new acquisition. You've got to follow certain procedures and take a few precautions at the point of purchase in order to assure yourself a lifetime of happiness with your art. The next chapter considers these procedures and precautions.

CHAPTER 18

The Buy: What It Involves and How to Make It

When you buy art, you can pay for it, take it home, display it, and forget about it—as many people do—but that would be very ill advised. Your purchase is a long-term investment, and you should be concerned about its future. Your relationship with this art is just beginning, and you want it to be a successful one. What you do now could easily affect the art's value—historical value, scholarly value, and dollar value—for generations to come (and for your descendants, in particular).

You must also be concerned about possible negative outcomes of your purchase. Two important points to consider are these: What if the art has been misrepresented to you in some way or, in a worst-case scenario, is not even by the artist it's supposed to be by? Obviously, you have to protect yourself. Attend to certain details now in order to maximize your enjoyment of the art, influence its resale value, and save yourself potential complications later.

PAYING FOR YOUR ART

Before looking to the future, let's deal with the present—the moment at which you actually pay for your art. You have two options here. You can either pay for it all at once, or you can pay for it over a period of time.

Many art galleries are amenable to allowing clients time to pay for their art, especially when the art is expensive. In these cases, collectors sometimes need to pay in several installments or make other special purchase arrangements. Even with moderately priced art, collectors may be given the option of making several payments over time, whether they need to or not.

The best procedure, assuming you can do it, is to pay the full price at the time of purchase. That way the transaction is complete and clean, you own the art outright, the seller has no further claim to it, and you have an immediate sense of how much money you've just spent. Even when you are offered optional payment plans, if you can afford to pay the total amount at once—which should be almost always—pay it.

Then again, if you are the type who likes to take advantage of terms just because they are available, that's fine too. Never use them as an excuse to overspend, though. A good procedure is not to ask for or insist on terms unless you need them. The best procedure is not to need them at all.

For you first-time buyers who are paying over time, know that art galleries do not charge interest. *Installment payments should never total more than the agreed-upon purchase price of the art, assuming you pay within a reasonable amount of time (usually three months or less).* If you need any longer than three months, you're probably spending too much and should consider tightening your budget and choosing another work of art that you can really afford.

When you buy art in installments, always make your payments on time. Dealers are quite flexible about sitting down with you and deciding how much you should pay by what dates. All you have to do is make those payments when you say you're going to.

Don't get a reputation for dragging things out. If you don't pay when you're supposed to, dealers will lose interest in extending you financial considerations, and, at worst, they may refuse to do any further business with you. They'll also tell other dealers to watch out for you, and that can seriously hurt your collecting. The art world is small, word travels fast, and no dealers like doing business with clients who don't pay on time.

DOCUMENTING YOUR PURCHASES

Formally document every work of art you buy. If problems ever arise with any art you own, proper written documentation leaves no question as to how the art was represented at the time of purchase. Never assume that verbal assurances are all that is necessary.

The First Document You Need Whenever You Buy Art is a Proof of Purchase—a Receipt. That receipt should accurately describe the art according to size, medium, artist, date executed, and any other pertinent details. It should be fully signed and dated by the seller.

The Second Document You Need is a Guarantee or Certificate of Authenticity Signed and Dated by Either the Seller, the Artist, or an Independent Authority Qualified to Make the Determination of Authenticity. This is a written statement confirming that the art in question is by the artist that the seller says it is by. Also stated should be any other facts relating to authenticity that have been told to you by the gallery.

The Third Document You Need, Especially When You Are Buying Art that is Not Brand New, is a Condition Report, that is, a Statement of the Art's

Condition at the Time You are Buying It. This document should either state that the art is in perfect original condition or else accurately describe any damage that the art has incurred over the years and specify whatever actions have been taken to repair it.

Along with this Documentation, You Need One More Thing: An Unconditional Money-Back Guarantee. Included in or attached to your receipt, authentication, and condition report must be a guarantee by the seller to return your purchase price in full at any point in the future should the art turn out to be other than it has been represented to be in any of those three documents. Sellers must take full financial responsibility for all statements they make about the art they sell.

Your receipt, authentication, condition statement, and money-back guarantee are the core of your documentation process, but also just a portion of the records you should keep. Start and maintain a file, beginning with these documents, on every piece of art you buy. Inside that file goes anything relating to that art or artist. Along with the core documents include relevant gallery and artist correspondences, newspaper or magazine articles, exhibition catalogues, invitations to openings, and so on. (If you have questions about how to acquire additional data for your files, review Chapter 13, "Provenance Is Profit.")

Never alter or destroy any of your file documents. Some collectors, for instance, throw away their original bills of sale because the art has increased in value since they bought it and they don't want anyone to know how little they originally paid for it. They believe that the receipt will decrease the art's value or that if they ever decide to sell, buyers will offer less if they find out the original cost. Nothing is further from the truth! The art is worth what it's worth no matter how little it originally sold for.

For example, when you see a Van Gogh painting, do you think about how little it sold for years ago? Do you think it would be worth less to a collector today because the collector knows that it sold for only a few dollars just after the turn of the century? Would you be interested in seeing an original receipt for a Van Gogh painting? Do you think that receipt would have historical significance and be worth money in and of itself? Of course. Case closed.

Summarizing, always include the following in your art files:

- The bill of sale

- The authentication

- The condition report

- A money-back guarantee protecting you if condition, authenticity, or any other data the seller gives you ever turns out to be other than represented

- Any incidental material that the seller gives you

- Any pertinent correspondences from the gallery, the artist, relatives of the artist, and so on

- Two good, clear photographs of the art, one in color and one in black and white (just in case the art ever gets stolen; black-and-white photographs reproduce better in newspapers, magazines, and other publications where you might want to make a theft known to the general public)

- Any material that you receive at any future date relating to that art or artist

- A current appraisal (less than three years old)

- Full instructions on what to do with the art should anything ever happen to you

Each file becomes a record of the art piece that it represents. It protects your investment. It is a source of information and details that you otherwise might forget. It educates and informs all interested parties. And, at any point in the future, that art's history can be traced right back to the day you bought it—and to an earlier time if you did extra research.

Above all, a file becomes part of the art itself and can be passed on to all subsequent owners of that art. The truth is that you won't be around forever to provide a verbal explanation of your art and the history behind it. Whoever owns the art after you will have the information you accumulated on hand to help explain the piece's value and significance. And should subsequent owners—your descendants, in particular—happen to be people who don't care that much about the art and would rather sell it than keep it, they'll have adequate data on hand to protect themselves from being taken advantage of by unscrupulous buyers.

RETURN AND EXCHANGE ARRANGEMENTS

Before beginning any discussion on returning or exchanging art, remember that art is not currency. Art galleries are not banks where you can exchange dollars for art and then, at some later date, return that art for any fraction of, either greater than, equal to, or less than, your initial purchase price. Return and exchange arrangements are not convenience services for transforming art into cash whenever you feel like it. You should, however, buy art only after you completely understand the return or exchange policy of the gallery selling it.

Many galleries offer what is called a *short-term return privilege* and provide it in writing. This privilege allows you to return the art for a full cash refund for a limited period of time immediately after your purchase. This limited period can range anywhere from one week to a month or two, depending on the gallery, during which time the art is returnable for whatever reason you have for not wanting to keep it, no questions asked. Of course, it is hoped by all involved that you will choose your art wisely and never have to take advantage of this option. Remember that if you have *any doubts whatsoever* about whether you really want to own a particular work of art, take it home on approval *before you buy it.*

Just about all galleries offer some form of *long-term return/exchange arrangement.* Such policies, which vary from gallery to gallery, concern how your art is to be handled if you decide to bring it back months, years, or even decades after you buy it. The two main options offered under such arrangements are taking your art back on consignment and selling it for you or allowing you to exchange it for gallery credit equal to your original purchase price.

Almost All Galleries Agree to Take Your Art Back on Consignment at Any Time and Sell it for You. This agreement saves you the trouble of having to resell the art yourself. The galleries display your art, offer it to their clients, and assume the responsibility of completing the sales transaction for you.

Not all consignment arrangements are the same. Understand what fees or commissions, if any, a gallery charges for reselling your art in this manner. Some galleries attempt to net you your original purchase price, some give you a portion of the profit if they sell your art for more than you paid for it, and others take a percentage of the selling price no matter what the art sells for. Whatever the arrangement, know what it is and get it in writing before you buy.

Consignment selling has one major drawback: There is no guarantee that your art will sell. Galleries have no problem offering consignment service because it involves no financial risk on their part. They only pay you if and when your art sells, not before.

Some dealers may lead you to believe that all you have to do is bring your art back and within a short period of time they'll resell it and you'll have your check, possibly with profit over your original purchase price. Don't believe this for a moment. Selling art on consignment takes time, and you may not recoup anywhere near the amount of money you originally paid. At worst, your art could sit for sale indefinitely without selling, in which case, you recoup nothing.

When galleries make consignment sound like a sure thing—like you can cash in your art at any time (usually with profit)—call them on it. Insist that they put their promises in writing and that they guarantee those returns. How many galleries do you think will be willing to go that far? You guessed it: *none*. The best approach is not to do business with these sorts of galleries in the first place.

A final note about consignment. Honest and experienced art dealers will tell you that, looking back on their years in business, they have sold some art that they would love to resell and other art that they would just as soon never see again. *No one can predict the financial future of any art or artist.* The passage of time is the ultimate determinant of how easy, difficult, or impossible reselling your art on consignment will be.

Here's a worst possible outcome scenario that puts consignment selling into its proper perspective. Suppose you buy a sculpture from a gallery that guarantees in writing to take it back on consignment at any point in the future. Ten years later, you ask the gallery to resell it for you. The gallery owner tells you that he'll take the sculpture back on consignment but he'll have an extremely difficult time selling it, if he can sell it at all, because the sculptor is no longer popular and has totally dropped from public view. He suggests that you'd be better off donating it to charity for a tax write-off. The final outcome here is that you receive none of your original cash outlay, and the consignment agreement is not even worth the piece of paper it's printed on.

Many Galleries Allow You the Option of Exchanging Your Art at Any Point in the Future for a Trade Value Equal to the Full Original Purchase Price. In this instance, a gallery credits that dollar amount toward a new purchase you make from their current stock at the time of the return or after. This arrangement gives you the luxury of returning your art effortlessly and at no cash loss should your tastes change or should you decide to upgrade your collection.

Exchange policies vary from gallery to gallery. Some galleries allow exchanges for anything in their stocks; others allow exchanges for only certain portions of their stocks. The most common arrangement allows you to exchange your art for any art that a gallery owns outright, but not for art that is there on consignment. If trade on consignments were allowed, a gallery would have to pay a consignor immediately upon receiving your art which would be basically the same as giving out a cash refund without taking any cash in. With rare exceptions, immediate cash is not issued to anyone when art is exchanged. Cash is paid out only after art sells.

Return or exchange policies at the same gallery can even vary from art piece to art piece, so understand what your options are on each individual work of art you buy. Never assume anything, and, as always, get whatever you are told in writing.

One final word: *Never abuse a return or exchange privilege.* Becoming known among dealers as someone who regularly returns art is bad for your reputation as a collector, and galleries will become reluctant to do any further business with you. When you buy art, be pretty sure you like it, pretty sure you can afford it, and pretty sure you're going to keep it.

ART BUYS THAT ARE LESS THAN IDEAL

Not all sellers provide buyers with proofs of authenticity, condition reports, data about the art they sell, consignment or trade-back arrangements, and other amenities. Some dealers sell art pretty much "as is" and have the attitude that once you buy it, you own it, and they want nothing more to do with it. This is their privilege and should not be taken as an indication that the art they sell is inferior in any way to "guaranteed" art.

The fewer assurances you get at the point of purchase, though, the more informed you have to be about what you are buying. When you're just starting out, the best procedure is to avoid buying art that comes with few or no guarantees and protections. Buy only from dealers who stand behind what they sell and take full responsibility for representing it properly. As you advance in your collecting, however, and learn more about what you're doing, you can become more adventurous in your buying habits.

Whenever you buy art under less-than-ideal circumstances, still record and file whatever information the seller gives you. With no authentication, condition report, or money-back guarantee, at least try to get a receipt that accurately describes the art as to artist, size, subject matter, and other particulars. Ask for a signed statement telling how the art was acquired and whatever additional facts the seller knows about it. If you are shown any documents relating to the art, ask that they be included in your purchase. When that's not possible, borrow them and make copies for your records.

Maintain a file even when you get no information from a seller. Write a statement yourself recounting the circumstances of your purchase, the purchase price, what the seller told you about the art, where it supposedly came from, and any other interesting details surrounding how the acquisition was made. This sort of documentation can eventually prove to be just as valuable and informative as the official material you get from established galleries.

Example 1: I once bought a painting from a dealer who gave me no guarantees on it. That was fine with me because I felt sure it was authentic and knew that for the size, subject matter, and quality of work, the price was fair. Several months later, however, another dealer saw the painting and told me she thought it could possibly be a forgery.

I decided to show it to an expert and see whether he would authenticate it for me. He wouldn't. He didn't come right out and say the picture was fake, but I got the idea that it (and I) obviously had problems. I contacted two other experts, and they gave me the same response: no go on the authentication.

I returned to the seller and explained my situation. He told me that although my plight was unfortunate, he was not willing to take the painting back and return my money. He had sold the art "as is"; I had bought it "as is." I was stuck with the painting. I, of course, stopped doing business with this dealer, but only after learning an expensive lesson—*get those guarantees.* No matter how much you think you know, you can always be fooled.

Example 2: An art collector told me about a time she tried to return a limited edition print to the gallery she had bought it from. When she bought the print, the gallery verbally guaranteed that she could have an immediate full cash refund if she returned it within two weeks. However, nothing was put in writing.

About a week after her purchase, the collector had second thoughts about the print and decided to return it. She brought it back to the gallery, explained her decision, and was told that the employee in charge of returns and exchanges was on vacation and would be back in several days. The person she was speaking with then attempted to convince her to keep the print. He said that the value was only going up, the artist was on the verge of having a major museum show, and so on. According to him, she was making a terribly wrong decision.

She insisted on returning it, however, and came back to the gallery several days later to complete the process. This time, she was introduced to the gallery owner, who talked to her about exchanging the print for one of equal value rather than taking the cash. She refused, demanded her money, and was finally allowed to "officially" return the print.

At that point the owner took the print back, but the woman still received no cash as she had been led to believe she would. He told her that restocking forms had to be processed and that she would have her money back within six to eight weeks.

The happy ending is that she did eventually get her money back. The lesson: *Get it in writing.* No matter what you are told and how wonderfully you are treated at the moment you buy, know the gallery policy and have it in writing.

A LOOK AHEAD

A unique kind of buying and selling situation in which art sellers regularly provide few or no guarantees on what they sell happens to be, oddly enough, extremely popular with collectors. The sellers do their best to properly represent what they have for sale, but in the end, you—the buyer—are the one charged with researching and evaluating any art you are interested in buying. You must decide whether or not it is authentic, what condition it is in, how significant it is, and what you think it's worth, because once you buy it, it's yours for keeps. The next chapter addresses the highest profile art arena of them all—an arena that no art book is complete without discussing—*the auction.*

CHAPTER 19

Action at the Auction

This chapter is placed last because that is exactly when beginning collectors should consider buying art at auction. This is not to say that auctions are bad places to buy art and that you should avoid them. Quite the contrary. Auctions are wonderful places to buy art, but only on the condition that you know what you're doing when you buy there.

More people than ever before are excited at the thought of buying art at auction. More people than ever before actually do buy art at auction. The great majority of auction-related publicity over recent years, much of it generated by the auction houses themselves, has been overwhelmingly pro-auction. In response to all this hype and hubbub, someone has to take the conservative, sober, and sensible approach to auctions. We'll do that here.

Anyone can attend auctions for the purpose of buying art. No law prohibits them. Auction houses have no knowledge or skill requirements for people who participate in and buy art at their sales. As far as these establishments are concerned, the more bidders they attract, the better.

Auctions are places where art experts, art dealers, and seasoned collectors go to buy art. Auctions are also places where beginning collectors who aren't too sure about what they are doing go to buy art. In fact, even people who have no idea what they are doing buy art at auction. The less experience buyers have, the more substantial the risks they take when they buy at auction. Many amateur auction patrons don't realize this.

The auctions we are primarily concerned with here are the less well known, secondary, and local firms. These smaller houses are the ones that conduct the great majority of sales nationwide and are also the ones where you are at the greatest risk when you buy art. In the substantial majority of cases, small auction house staffs are not qualified to oversee and accurately evaluate every piece of art that is placed up for sale at their establishments.

This chapter is also applicable to some of the major houses, in spite of the fact that they are a great deal more selective in what they sell. Even though they employ qualified experts to carefully examine and screen all art before it is accepted for sale, you still take big chances buying at these establishments if you don't know what you're doing. The very best auction houses (see Appendix 3) do employ experts who can guide you, but this is by far the exception, rather than the rule. *No matter what caliber of auction house you patronize, the great bulk of the responsibility for knowing what you are buying and how to go about buying it always lies with you.*

AUCTIONS VERSUS ART GALLERIES

Buying art at auction is different from buying at galleries. Sure, the art you see at auction looks basically the same as the art you see at galleries. It is often attractively presented, displayed, and lit, and it hangs on the walls and sits on the pedestals just like art gallery art does. But that's where the similarities end.

Auctions Are Less Specialized Than Art Galleries. For example, you can find galleries dealing in types of art as specific as Minnesota art and artists, American art from the 1930s and 1940s, contemporary French sculpture, and so on. Specialized galleries are experts at what they sell; they spend all their working hours focusing exclusively on that area of art and, as a result, are able to provide their clients with the maximum amount of knowledge about whatever specific art they happen to deal in.

Auctions, on the other hand, do not specialize and thus do not provide that degree of knowledge and background information on what they sell. The great majority of auction houses accept whatever people bring them, display it all together in the same room, and let the potential buyers figure out what's what. You can see anything from seventeenth-century portraits to contemporary abstracts, from Minnesota landscapes to Paris street scenes, all up for sale at the same auction.

Auction houses do the best they can with whatever resources they have on hand to determine whether the art that people consign for sale is authentic, but beyond that they take few of the pains that private galleries do (such as determining how good the art examples are, whether they are typical or atypical of the artists' work, what periods in the artists' developments they represent, whether they are done in the artists' preferred mediums, and so on).

Because Auctions Accept Such a Wide Range of Art, They Generally Do Not Present Consistent Quality the Way Galleries Do. Galleries pick and choose specific pieces for their clientele. Auctions do this to a certain extent, especially the best houses, but most tend to be less selective. Once again, they throw everything together and let the buyer decide what's great, good, and not so good. After all, auctions are not in the art gallery business, they are in the business of selling merchandise for their consignors.

Auctions Rarely Invest Money in What They Sell. This no-risk situation for the auction houses gives them a special advantage over art galleries, which normally buy their art outright, and gives you still another reason to be cautious about auction buying. Because auctions do not pay for what they accept on consignment, they can take chances and accept marginal items that may or may not do well at their sales. Merchandise that does not sell is simply returned to the consignors, and the auction firms are no worse off for their efforts. (Incidentally, some major firms do advance cash on important consignments, but that practice involves only a minute percentage of art sold at auction.)

You Have No Return or Exchange Privileges When Buying at Auction. Unlike buying at galleries, when you buy art at auction, it's yours for good. All sales are final. Make sure you like a piece before you buy it, because if you change your mind, the only way to get your money back is to place it back up for sale and hope for the best.

A Most Important Difference Between Auctions and Galleries is that Auctions Provide Few, if any, Guarantees on What They Sell. The best houses do offer what amount to limited guarantees of authenticity. Depending on the firm and the state they are located in, an auction house may allow you to return merchandise for a certain period of time after it is sold, ranging anywhere from thirty days to as long as five years in exceptional cases. In order for an auction firm to take the art back, however, you must conclusively prove, with expert testimony, that it was not properly represented. When a limited guarantee ends, auctions are no longer legally bound to accept returns, although many established firms still take them back when buyers present strong enough cases and insist on having their money refunded.

Whenever you attend an auction, familiarize yourself with their statements of policy called the "Conditions of Sale." You usually see these conditions listed at the beginning of auction catalogues or posted on auction house walls. If you can't find them, ask to see them. *Read the conditions word for word.* Once you become familiar with such conditions you will realize just how cautious you have to be when you buy at auction as opposed to at a gallery. The conditions state exactly what the auction house is responsible for—which is not too much—and what you are responsible for—which is just about everything.

For example, suppose you are at an auction where the auctioneer states that the next item to go up for bidding is a painting signed "John Doe." The auctioneer means *exactly* what he says—that he is selling a painting signed "John Doe"—and nothing more. He is not guaranteeing that the painting is by Doe. Maybe it is, maybe it isn't. All he is doing is stating the fact that it happens to have "John Doe" signed on it. Are the painting and signature authentic? That's for you to decide.

The average auction sale is the ultimate arena for the policy "Let the buyer beware." Auctions are not retail art galleries that provide fully documented, fully condition-inspected, fully researched, and fully guaranteed products to the public. Never confuse the two.

COMMON MISCONCEPTIONS ABOUT AUCTIONS

Some of the reasons why so many art buyers find auctions so attractive are not really valid at all. Clearing up a few commonly held misconceptions will help place auction buying in its proper perspective.

The Belief that Auctions Are Where You Go To Find Bargains Is Not True. The chances of your getting a bona fide bargain at auction are remote. First of all, auction houses want everything they sell to sell for as much money as possible. When they receive art on consignment that they suspect might have value, they research it. If they don't have the capacity to research it, they do the next best thing, which is to publicize the fact that they have it for sale as widely as possible and do whatever is necessary to catch the attention of buyers who do know how to research it. All they have to do is reach two buyers who know how much the art is worth (which is almost always accomplished with ease) and then let the bidding begin. That art ends up selling for a respectable price.

Another reason for the lack of bargains is that just about the only person who wants to see art auction cheaply is you, the potential buyer. Everyone else wants to see it sell for as much money as possible. The auctioneer wants high prices because that means good profits and good publicity for the auction house. High prices also mean more business for the auction house because potential consignors are encouraged to consign merchandise. Consignors naturally want to get as much money as possible for what they consign. Collectors who already own works by artists whose art is up for sale at auction want that art to sell high, because strong sales increase the value of the art in their collections. And don't forget the rest of the art community. They want high prices because that indicates a healthy and active art market in general. So it's you against the world.

In spite of all this, people continue to shop auctions for bargains, an ironic consequence of which is that prices on second-rate works of art have increased substantially in recent years. Many experts believe that this is

178

primarily due to inexperienced collectors not recognizing that the art they are buying "so cheaply" is not very good and not necessarily worth the "bargain prices" they think they are paying for it.

The Belief that Auction Prices are Always Lower than Art Gallery Prices is not True. Auction art does not always sell at wholesale or below retail. Some art sells for more money at auction than it does anywhere else. In fact, certain art dealers regularly monitor auctions and cash in on the phenomenon by playing to whatever the current auction buying frenzies are. They consign a continuing flow of the exact types of art that bidders are inclined to pay strong prices for at any particular auction.

The Belief that Art is Worth What Auction Houses Think It Will Sell for is not True. Many auctions either include estimated selling prices in their sale catalogues or tell you how much they expect certain items to sell for. Although many such estimates are accurate, some are too high and others are too low. You take your financial health into your own hands when you bid on art based only on auction house estimates.

Why are estimates sometimes too high? There are a number of reasons. An auction house may place an unrealistically high estimate on a certain piece of art as a favor to a client who regularly consigns merchandise, or a research error may lead a staff person to overvalue a work of art, or the auction house may be fishing for a buyer to pay at or near a deliberately overestimated price, and so on.

Why are estimates sometimes too low? Again, for various reasons. Research errors may be to blame. Other times, auctions purposely put low estimates on art in order to attract buyers to their sales. The theory here (which does seem to work) is that once people are physically at a sale, they tend to buy even if they don't get the bargains they thought they would.

The Belief that No One Ever Overpays for Art at Auction is not True. One reason why people overpay is that they mistakenly accept pre-sale estimates as gospel. When two or more bidders believe that unrealistically high estimates are realistic, the art sells for more than it's worth. Other reasons why people overpay usually involve their bidding for reasons other than wanting to own art (this is discussed in the next section).

The Belief that Only People Who Know Nothing About Art Attend Small-Town, Offbeat, or Country Auctions is not True. This is a misconception for those of you who fantasize about finding Rembrandts for pennies at backwoods sales. Pros monitor just about every auction, no matter how remote it is. When something good comes up for sale, people who know how much it's worth and are willing to pay good money for it somehow manage to find out about it.

Assuming you know how to evaluate and research a work of art you see at auction, you still have to know what to do next and how to act at the sale itself. A lot more goes on at auction sales, in a psychological sense, than people innocently holding up their bidding cards and buying art. Within the ranks of the bidders there are many different forces at work. All kinds of people bid on and buy art at auction for all kinds of reasons.

Experienced, rational buyers make up the large majority of auction bidders and are also the most predictable. Such buyers research whatever art they are interested in buying and bid in an informed, calculated manner. They know exactly what they want and how much they are willing to pay for it. If they get it, fine. If they don't, they wait until next time.

At the other end of the rationality continuum are those few bidders who go completely wild and are victims of what is often described as "auction fever." They bid as much for thrills, excitement, and victory over the competition as they do for the art itself. For them, nothing quite equals the emotional charge of raising their bidding cards skyward in the midst of crowded rooms, beating out fellow buyers, and taking home their "trophies." The most excessive among them decide they must own certain items no matter what the cost.

Other less common types of bidders and bidding styles include the following:

- *People who purposely bid art up in order to inflate the value of their own collections.* For example, an individual or gallery that owns a lot of art by one artist places a piece of that art up at auction and has friends or acquaintances deliberately bid it up to a higher price than it has ever sold for before. The impressive auction record becomes public knowledge, and people who see it without understanding how it came about mistakenly conclude that the artist's work is increasing in value and collectibility.

- *People who bid because they see an arch rival bidding.* Such bidders may not even be interested in owning the art or care how much they have to pay for it. All they care about is competing.

- *People who bid on a piece of art only when they see specific dealers or experienced collectors bid on it first.* They respect those dealers or collectors and figure that anything these pros think is worth bidding on must be good. As an aside, dealers and collectors who are victimized by people watching their every move often counter this problem by bidding over the phone or by hiring confederates to bid in their places.

- *People who bid to impress spouses, friends, relatives, or business associates.* The art is always secondary here.

- *People who bid on art they never intend to own and do so only to see how high they can push up the final selling prices before safely dropping out of the action.* The few bidders who do this are usually skilled auction buyers who know just when to quit and rarely, if ever, get stuck with anything they don't want. They could almost be called shills except for the fact that they have no connection with auction houses and do what they do entirely for their own amusement.

You see that plenty goes on at auction besides simple buying of art. People can bid on whatever they want for whatever reason they want to and pay as much as they feel like paying for it. What does this mean for you? That you've got to be absolutely confident of your intentions and your knowledge of what you are bidding on before getting involved.

AUCTION PLUS POINTS: WHY BUY ART AT AUCTION?

In spite of all these cautions and warnings, auctions can be great places to buy art. Any experienced auction buyer will tell you this. *If you know what you are doing, and this is a big "if," you can buy wonderful works of art for reasonable prices at auction.* You can even find bargains if you're really skilled at researching, setting your limits, and bidding.

To Begin With, Auctions Sell a Substantial Amount of High-Quality Art Fresh Out of Private Collections. Private sellers do not always have the time, the inclination, or the know-how to sell their art to galleries and, as a result, choose the easy auction option. Corporations, businesses, museums, historical societies, and other institutions further contribute to the fascinating array of art that auction houses continually offer at their public sales.

Auctions are About the Only Places Where You Can Compete for Art Directly with Art Dealers. Auctions are free and open public forums where anyone who wants to has the identical opportunity to bid and buy alongside anyone else. Unlike in many other buying situations, at auctions dealers have no special advantages over collectors (such as special trade discounts, exclusive viewing privileges, and so on).

All Collectors are Treated Equally at Auction. Private galleries, on the other hand, frequently offer their latest arrivals to their longest standing and best clients first. They sell plenty of art before the general public ever has a chance to see it. At a gallery as a first-time or second-time buyer, you either have to choose from what's left over or wait until you move up in a gallery owner's customer hierarchy before being able to take first pick of the best new arrivals. At auction you have that pick immediately.

The Fact that Auctions Sell Art "as is" Gives You Reason to be Cautious in Your Buying, but the "as is" Situation Can Also Work in Your Favor. Perfectly good-quality art may be placed up at auction poorly framed, with minor damage, dirty, or with other easily rectifiable problems. Dealers buy this art at wholesale prices, clean it up, frame it, and mark it up to full retail after providing those services. You can buy that same art at auction prices, have it repaired, cleaned, and framed yourself, and save money over the extra profit margin you would normally pay galleries to do it for you.

The Fact that Auctions do not Specialize Can Be Viewed as a Plus Point Rather than a Drawback. Because auctions accept a much greater variety of art than galleries do, they provide you with regular opportunities to view different and unusual pieces that you would not ordinarily see for sale anywhere else. You can use these opportunities to broaden your general knowledge of art and possibly even expand your collecting horizons.

Auctions Tend to be More Open with Respect to Supplying Provenance than Galleries Are. Many auction houses will contact consignors at buyers' requests to see whether they mind revealing their identities, whether they are willing to provide written statements or other information about the art they consigned, and so on. Galleries tend to be much more protective about their sources. Especially when private dealers acquire art at bargain prices or are supplied from regularly producing sources, they are not interested in naming names.

At Auction, You Often Have a Longer Time to Deliberate Over What You See for Sale Than You do at Galleries. Most auction firms announce their sales anywhere from several weeks to a month or more in advance. This gives you ample time to research art you like; view it repeatedly during the pre-sale period; and decide how much you really like it, whether you want to own it, and how much you are willing to pay for it. Private galleries, on the other hand, frequently offer brief options to buy, sometimes lasting only a day or two, before they resume offering their art to other clients. This sort of pressure situation is never in the buyer's favor.

Suppose you want to buy art at auction at some point in your collecting career. First-timers have to start somewhere, and no matter what type of auction you intend to patronize, the learning procedures are basically the same.

When You're Just Starting Out, Stick with Established Auction Houses that have Experience Selling Art. Be wary of traveling auctions, special art auctions conducted by firms that do not regularly handle art, "bargain art" or liquidation auctions, and other out-of-the-ordinary, transient, or irregularly held sales. The risks to beginners are simply too great at events like these. Attend offbeat sales without participating in order to broaden your knowledge of what auctions are all about, but as for actually bidding, wait until you've had more experience bidding at established auctions.

The First Step in Learning About Auctions is to Preview and Attend as Many Sales as you can *Without Bidding*. Research any art that interests you just as though you were actually going to buy it. Do standard artist and art research, evaluate prices, and decide the maximum amounts you would be willing to pay if you were actually bidding. Attend the sales themselves, feel the excitement, watch what happens, pay attention to how the auctioneers offer the merchandise and how the buyers respond, get accustomed to the rapid pace at which the lots sell, imagine yourself making bids, and acclimate yourself to the pressurized atmosphere of the sales room. Once you feel reasonably comfortable and familiar with how auctions progress, you're ready to seriously compete against other bidders and buy art.

An Essential Rule to Follow at any Auction Where You Intend to Bid is This: Always Attend the Preview and Spend Plenty of Time Studying the Art While You're There. The preview is the most important part of any sale because it is here that you have a chance to view the art firsthand, examine its every detail, inspect it for condition or authenticity problems, and decide how much you like it and whether or not you want to own it. *Never* bid on or buy art that you have not previewed beforehand.

At Any Preview, Study All of the Art for Sale. Even if you don't like a piece, spend at least a little time looking at it and learning about it. This exercise will increase your knowledge of art in general. After you've taken a preliminary look around, then start focusing in on the specific works of art that appeal to you the most.

Carefully Study Your Favorites for Ten or Fifteen Minutes Each, Come Back in an Hour and Study Them Again for Ten or Fifteen More Minutes

Each, Come Back the Next Day and Repeat the Procedure, and so on. The more you look at your choices, the better you get to know them and understand how strongly you feel about owning them. Make sure you like the way they look and really want to own them, because once you buy them, they're yours.

Determine the Condition of Any Art You Intend to Bid On. Take it off the wall or remove it from its pedestal, turn it over, lift it up, look at it under a magnifying glass—do whatever you have to do in order to examine its every detail. Note whatever problems the art has.

Study All Information the Auction House Provides About the Art. This may be in the form of a listing in an auction catalogue, a sheet of paper you are handed as you arrive at the preview, or in some other form. Copy anything you cannot take from the auction house, and keep it on hand for future reference.

Have the Auction Staff Person or Persons in Charge of Art Tell You Everything They Know About the Art You Are Interested In. See if the staff person is aware of any condition problems. Ask also if that person knows where the art came from, whether any official documents accompany the art, why it was consigned, and any details you might need to evaluate the art. Find out everything you can. Write down any pertinent details, and save them for later reference.

After Attending the Preview and Gathering Information, Research, Research, Research! Find out everything you possibly can about the art and its artists from sources outside the auction house according to the procedures outlined in Part III of this book. Study biographical information about the artists. Determine the significance of the art. Evaluate the artists' price structures according to procedures outlined in Chapter 17. Never rely solely on the pre-sale estimates the auction house gives you; independently confirm any other statements the auction house has made to you either verbally or in the sale catalogue.

Based on Your Research, Decide What Your Maximum Bids Will Be and *Stay With Those Bids Right Through to the Close of the Bidding.* Whether or not your high bids relate to the auction house estimates or what the art eventually sells for, do not change your mind at the last minute. The moment you reach your limit on any one bid, drop your card and wait for the next item you're interested in to come up for sale.

Controlling yourself during bidding is especially important if you are an inexperienced bidder. Novices tend to get carried away at the last moment, throw their research results to the wind, and bid just to buy something no matter what they have to pay for it. In the heat of a crowded, fast-paced auction sale, a few seconds of indiscretion can cost you big dollars. So don't be upset if you come away empty-handed. You'll find plenty more works of art to bid on at future sales.

If You are Nervous About Buying at Auction and Want to Work Your Way into it More Gradually, Hire a No-Conflict Resource You Know, Trust, and Can Confide in to Inspect, Research, and Even Bid on the Art for You. Attend the preview together, examine and discuss the art, research it, and decide what to do based primarily on this expert's professional opinion. The best auction houses offer consultation services, but even so, hiring independent, unbiased experts is a more sensible way. Most experts perform this service either for a flat fee or for a percentage of the final selling price, usually ranging between 4 and 10 percent.

Asking independent experts for their opinions without paying them can sometimes be hazardous to your bidding. Those authorities can conceivably become your adversaries when they are under no obligation to work on your behalf. For example, your innocent questions may call an expert's attention to a work of art that he or she did not notice initially and would have overlooked entirely if you hadn't asked about it. The expert might decide that you're on to something good and end up bidding against you.

Example 1: Experienced dealers and collectors know to attend all auctions where art they are interested in bidding on is being sold. They appear at the sales ready to bid regardless of how high the pre-sale estimates are, how much experts expect the art to sell for, and how dim the prospects seem for getting the art at the prices they're willing to pay. In the auction business, you never know what's going to sell for what until it actually sells.

A friend of mine likes to relate a story about a painting he saw at an auction preview. It had a pre-sale estimate of $20,000 to $40,000. Interest in the picture was strong, and the general word among those in the know was that the final selling price was expected to be somewhere between $40,000 and $50,000. Although this collector was willing to bid as high as $30,000, certainly a respectable amount of money, he had pretty much given up any hope of getting the painting. Nevertheless, he attended the sale.

When he arrived, he found the auction room nearly empty. Even so, the other works of art were still selling at substantial prices—nothing was selling terribly low. He didn't have high hopes for being the winning bidder on his favorite painting, but now he felt he at least had an outside chance because of the low attendance. When the painting came up for sale, he sat silently without bidding and prepared to watch it sell for well over $30,000. To his

185

surprise, bidding abruptly stopped at $18,000. He couldn't believe it. He raised his card and got the painting for $19,000—almost 40 percent less than what he would have gladly paid and less than half of what the experts had expected it to sell for.

He explains his good fortune as follows. Everyone who was interested in the painting was so sure it would sell high that no one left any absentee bids on it and no one attended the sale. Everyone thought everyone else would be bidding on it when, in fact, they had all psyched each other out. The only person left who was willing to pay any serious money for it was him.

Whether or not his explanation is right, such unexpected turns of events happen all the time at auctions. If you see art you like at a preview, never assume it's out of your reach until the final bid is made and the hammer falls.

CONCLUSION

You now have all the basic tools you need to identify, select, research, and buy good-quality art at fair prices. All you have to do is follow the various directives as they have been outlined here and avoid taking shortcuts. This may seem a little time-consuming at first, but once you get the hang of things, you will be able to progress smoothly from your first contact with any work of art that happens to catch your eye right on through to the final purchase— and all within a matter of a day or two at the very most.

Congratulations, good luck, and buy art smart!

Appendixes

1: Art Periodicals

Apollo: Apollo Magazine Ltd., 22 Davies St., London W1Y ILH, England. Art articles and advertisements relate primarily to period European art.

Art & Antiques: Allison Publications, Inc., 89 Fifth Avenue, New York, NY 10003. Art articles and advertisements relate primarily to American and European period and contemporary art.

Art & Auction: Auction Guild, 250 West 57th St., New York, NY 10019. Art articles and advertisements relate primarily to American and European period art, with a smattering of contemporary art. The focus of this magazine is on the world auction market.

Art in America: Brant Publications, 980 Madison Avenue, 3d Floor, New York, NY 10021. Articles and advertisements relate to international contemporary art with the focus being on contemporary art in America.

Artforum: Artforum International Magazine, Inc., 65 Bleecker St., New York, NY 10012. Articles and advertisements relate primarily to international contemporary and avant garde art.

Artnews: Artnews Associates, 48 West 38th St., New York, NY 10018. Articles and advertisements relate primarily to international contemporary art.

Connaissance des Arts: Societe Française de Promotion Artistique, 25 rue de Ponthieu, 75008 Paris, France. Art articles and advertisements relate primarily to period European art.

The Magazine Antiques: Brandt Publishers, Inc., 980 Madison Ave, New York, NY 10021. Art articles and advertisements relate primarily to pre-1940 American art and artists. This is the best resource for advertisements of major American art dealers who specialize in period American art. Some European dealers also advertise.

> *Note:* There are numerous other national and international periodicals that relate to art. Check with art dealers, collectors, art librarians, and curators to see which publications best suit your needs.

2: Art Reference Sources

ARTIST INDEXES

Art Index: The H. W. Wilson Company, Bronx, N.Y.; published quarterly. This publication indexes articles and advertisements of art periodicals from around the world. It is extremely comprehensive and can be quite valuable not only in locating information about specific artists but also in locating illustrations of works by those artists and names of dealers who deal in their art. All major art libraries subscribe to this publication. Use it whenever you get the chance.

Busse, Joachim. *Internationales Handbuch Aller Maler und Bildhauer Des 19, Jahrhunderts:* Busse Kunst Dokumentation GmbH, Wiesbaden, 1977. This important and comprehensive index contains the names of several hundred thousand nineteenth-century painters and sculptors and is particularly strong on European artists.

Castagno, John. *Artists as Illustrators: An International Directory With Signatures and Monograms, 1800–Present:* Scarecrow Press, Metuchen, N.J., 1989. If you collect illustration art, particularly by American illustrators, this book is for you. It's also good for European illustrators.

Havlice, P. P. *Index to Artistic Biography:* Scarecrow Press, Metuchen, N.J., 1973, 2 vols.; first supplement, 1981. This index is best for researching American artists but is also good for European. Dealers and collectors will tell you that this is one of the more frequently consulted art reference indexes. Use it regularly.

Havlice, P. P. *World Painting Index:* Scarecrow Press, Metuchen, N.J., 1977, 2 vols.; first supplement, 2 vols., 1982. Use this reference whenever you want to locate publications that contain illustrations of art by whatever artists you happen to be researching.

McNeil, Barbara. *Artist Biographies Master Index:* Gale Research Company, Detroit, Mich., 1986. This index lists not only artists, but also photographers, craftspeople, illustrators, designers, graphic artists, and architects. Always an important index to check, especially when you are researching less well known artists. This index is strong on American artists and adequate on European artists.

Mallett, D. T. *Mallett's Index of Artists:* Peter Smith, New York, 1948, 2 vols. This index is a little out of date, but it is still a worthwhile one to check if you are collecting art by artists who were active before 1950. This index is strong on American artists and adequate on European artists.

Meyer, George H. *Folk Artists Biographical Index:* Gale Research Company, Detroit, Mich., 1987. It is essential to check this index if you collect American folk art (but not necessary to check it otherwise). Lists artists who were active from the seventeenth century right on through to the present.

ARTIST ENCYCLOPEDIAS

Benezit, Emmanuel. *Dictionnaire critique et documentaire des peintres, sculpteurs, desinateurs et graveurs, de tous le temps et tous le pays:* Librarie Grund, Paris, 1976, 10 vols. Includes artists from around the world; is particularly strong on European artists.

Bihalji-Merin, Oto. *World Encyclopedia of Naive Art:* Scala/Philip Wilson, Yugoslavia, 1985. If you collect folk or naive art, this reference is for you. Contains numerous color illustrations.

Comanducci, A. M. *Dizionario illustrato del Pittori, Disegnatori e Incisori Italiani Moderni e Contemporanei:* Luigi Patuzzi Editore, Milan, 1970, 5 vols. It is essential to check this encyclopedia if you collect art by modern Italian artists. Contains numerous illustrations.

Gesualdo, Vincente. *Enciclopedia del Arte en America:* Bibliografica Omeba, Buenos Aires, 1968, 5 vols. This is the encyclopedia for you if you collect art by Latin American artists. Contains black-and-white illustrations.

Scheen, Pieter A. *Lexicon Nederlandse Beeldende Kunstenaars, 1750–1950:* Gravenhage, Netherlands, 1969, 2 vols. This encyclopedia lists artists who were active in the Netherlands between 1750 and 1950.

Thieme, Ulrich, and Felix Becker. *Allgemeines Lexikon der Bildenden Kunstler:* Seemann, Leipzig, 1908–1950, 37 vols. This is the best and most comprehensive artist encyclopedia. It lists artists from around the world who were active from the earliest times up through 1950, and it is particularly strong on Europeans. Many times you will find an artist listed here who is not listed anywhere else.

Vollmer, Hans. *Allgemeines Lexicon der Bildenden Kunstler des 20, Jahrhunderts:* E. A. Seamann, Germany, 1960. Check this reference if you collect art by twentieth-century artists. It includes artists from around the world but is particularly strong on Europeans.

Cummings, Paul. *Dictionary of Contemporary American Artists:* St. Martins Press, Inc., New York, 1988. Good for researching American artists who began their careers after 1950.

Emanuel, Muriel. *Contemporary Artists:* St. Martins Press, Inc., New York, 1983. This dictionary is a standard for researching contemporary artists from around the world. Most useful when researching artists who began their careers after 1950.

Falk, Peter H. *Who Was Who in American Art:* Sound View Press, Madison, Conn., 1985. This is the best single reference for researching American artists who were active at any time from the last quarter of the nineteenth century through the middle part of the twentieth century. It is a condensation of artist listings from a series of books published between those years called *American Art Annuals* and the first four volumes of another series called *Who's Who in American Art* (see next section in this appendix, "Art Annuals and Directories," for more complete listings on these annuals).

Groce, George C., and David H. Wallace. *The New York Historical Society's Dictionary of Artists in America, 1564–1860:* Yale University Press, New Haven, Conn., 1957. This is the best single reference for researching American artists who were active at any time before 1860.

Johnson, J., and A. Greutzner. *The Dictionary of British Artists, 1880–1940:* Antique Collectors' Club, England, 1984. The title of this book is self-explanatory.

Krantz, Les. *American Artists: An Illustrated Survey of Leading Contemporary Americans:* Facts on File Publications, New York, 1985. Best for researching American artists who began their careers after 1950. Each listing contains descriptive statements about the artist's art in addition to the usual biographical data. The book is also illustrated.

Opitz, Glenn B. *Mantle Fielding's Dictionary of American Painters, Sculptors & Engravers:* Apollo Book, Poughkeepsie, N.Y., 1986. This book was once a standard art business reference, but it has since been superceded by more specialized and comprehensive references. Still a good reference to check, though. Primarily covers American artists who were active before 1940.

Opitz, Glenn B. *Dictionary of American Sculptors: 18th Century to the Present:* Apollo Book, Poughkeepsie, N.Y., 1984. If you collect American sculpture, this book is an absolute necessity. Has illustrations at the rear of the book.

Petteys, Chris. *Dictionary of Women Artists:* G. K. Hall, Boston, 1985. This well-researched dictionary contains information about women artists from around the world who were active before 1900. It also has a great bibliography.

Wood, Christopher. *The Dictionary of Victorian Painters:* Antique Collectors' Club, England, 1981. Lists British artists who were active between 1837 and 1901. Contains about 500 illustrations that cover the full scope of Victorian painting. Excellent reference.

Zellman, Michael D. *300 Years of American Art:* Wellfleet Press, Secaucus, N.J., 1987, 2 vols. This dictionary lists over 800 American painters and covers the time period from the late seventeenth century through the mid-twentieth century. Artists listings are comprehensive. Each contains at least one color illustration, and many also contain market information which, unfortunately, is already well outdated. This is one of the best American art reference books ever published.

ART ANNUALS AND DIRECTORIES

American Art Annual: American Federation of Arts, Washington, D.C., 1898–1936, 33 vols. This is the preeminent source of information about American artists who were active during this time period. Any major art library has the majority of AAA's in its reference section.

Art & Auction Annual International Directory for Collectors: Special issue of *Art & Auction* magazine published by Auction Guild, 250 West 57th St., New York, NY 10019. This all-purpose reference includes information about antiques dealers, art galleries, auction houses, antiques shows, art services (art book dealers, art consultants, shippers, conservators, framers, etc.), art associations, art fairs, and so on.

Art in America Annual Guide to Galleries, Museums, Artists: Special issue of *Art in America* magazine published by Brant Publications, 980 Madison Ave., 3d Floor, New York, NY 10021. Contains information about art galleries, museums, artists, private dealers, print dealers, and art catalogues. Focus is on contemporary American artists, but also includes information about a number of resources for collectors of period American art.

International Directory of Arts: Art Address Verlag Muller GmbH & Co. KG, Frankfurt, Germany, 2 vols.; currently in its 19th edition, 1989–1990. This reference is extremely comprehensive, and even though it includes worldwide resources, it is primarily for collectors of European art. It lists museums, universities, artists, art galleries, auctions, book publishers, periodicals, booksellers, and so on.

Who's Who in American Art: R. R. Bowker, New York; published since 1936 and currently in its 18th volume. This is the best source of basic information about American artists who have been active at any time between 1936 and the present. The more recent editions of *Who's Who* also list art curators with major museums, important art scholars, librarians with major institutions, art writers, art critics, and other art-related personalities.

ART AUCTION RECORDS AND PRICE GUIDES

Beyard, Ernest R. *Art at Auction in America:* Krexpress, Silver Spring, Md., 1989. At $27.95, this is the first popularly priced annual auction record compendium ever; pocket sized.

Currier, William T. *Currier's Price Guide to American Artists, 1645–1945, at Auction:* Currier Publications, Brockton, Mass., 1990. Best pocket price guide to American artists. Covers over 7,000 artists.

Currier, William T. *Currier's Price Guide to European Artists, 1545–1945, at Auction:* Currier Publications, Brockton, Mass., 1990. Contains information on over 12,000 artists.

Currier, William T. *Currier's Price Guide to American and European Prints at Auction:* Currier Publications, Brockton, Mass., 1990. The only pocket price guide to prints. Covers over 2,500 artists.

Davenport, R. J. *Davenport's Art Reference and Price Guide:* Davenport's Art Reference, Ventura, Calif., 1990; 2 vols. This book can also be used as an art index. It lists over 75,000 artists, includes basic biographical as well as price information about the artists, and, like an index, often refers you to other references where you can locate further information. Watch out when the price information is given in the form of a price range instead of as specific auction sales results. The price ranges tend to be inaccurate.

Gordon, Martin. *Gordon's Print Price Annual:* Editions Publisol, New York, 1990. This auction record compendium is published annually and is the best reference for auction records for prints.

Hislop, Richard. *Art Quest:* Art Sales Index, Ltd, Weybridge, Surrey, England. This is an on-line database containing information about 950,000 works of art by 95,000 artists that have sold at auction since 1970 and is a must for serious collectors. For more information, write to Art Sales Index, Ltd., 1 Thames St., Weybridge, Surrey KT13 8JG, England, or call (0932) 856-426.

Hislop, Richard. *Art Sales Index:* Art Sales Index, Ltd., Weybridge, Surrey, England, 1990, 2 vols. This auction record compendium is published annually. It is extremely comprehensive and is the compendium of choice of many art dealers and collectors. It is the best guide for European artist auction records and is also excellent for American artist records.

Hislop, Richard. *The 1990 Picture Price Guide to the UK Art Market:* Art Sales Index, Ltd, Weybridge, Surrey, England, 1990. Best pocket price guide for researching European artists, particularly British. Information on nearly 13,000 artists.

McKittrick, Rosemary and Michael. *McKittrick's Art Price Guide:* McKittrick Fine Arts, Sewickley, Pa., 1990. This annual auction record compendium is a relatively new entry into the compendium market. It is strongest on American artist auction results and catalogues sales results from many lesser American auction houses that most other compendiums don't cover. It also sells for about half the price of the more expensive compendiums.

Meyer, E. *International Auction Records:* Archer Fields, Inc., New York, 1990. This auction record compendium is published annually and is the compendium of choice for dealers and collectors of more expensive works of art. Each volume is divided into separate sections for paintings, drawings, prints, and sculptures.

Theran, Susan. *Leonard's Annual Price Index of Art Auctions:* Auction Index, Ltd., West Newton, Mass., 1990. This auction record compendium is published annually and is strongest on auction results for American artists. It catalogues sales results from many lesser American auction houses.

Theran, Susan. *The Official Price Guide to Fine Art:* The House of Collectibles, New York, 1987. This guide provides more accurate price information about American artists than about European artists. It is already a little out of date, however, and if it is not revised soon, it will cease to be of value.

Ritzenthaler, C., and F. Van Wilder. *L'Officiel Des Arts:* Editions Van Wilder, France, 1989. This auction record compendium is published semiannually and is strongest on European artists, particularly French.

3: Significant American Auction Houses

Adam A. Weschler and Son, Inc., 909 E St. NW, Washington, D.C. 20004; (202) 628-1281

Butterfield and Butterfield, 220 San Bruno Ave., San Francisco, CA 94103; (415) 861-7500

C. G. Sloan & Co., Inc., 4950 Wyaconda Rd., Rockville, MD 20852; (202) 468-4911

Chicago Art Galleries, 20 West Hubbard St., Chicago, IL 60610; (312) 645-0686

Christie, Manson & Woods, International, 502 Park Ave., New York, NY 10022; (212) 546-1000

DuMouchelle Art Gallery, 409 East Jefferson Ave., Detroit, MI 48226; (313) 963-6255

Freeman/Fine Arts of Philadelphia, 1808 Chestnut St., Philadelphia, PA 19103; (215) 563-9275

James R. Bakker, Inc., 370 Broadway, Cambridge, MA 02139; (617) 864-7067

Leslie Hindman Auctioneers, 215 West Ohio St., Chicago, IL 60610; (312) 670-0010

Milwaukee Auction Galleries, Ltd., 318 North Water St., Milwaukee, WI 53202; (414) 271-1105

Mystic Fine Arts, 47 Holmes St., Mystic, CT 06355; (203) 572-8141

Phillips Son & Neale, 406 East 79th St., New York, NY 10021; (212) 570-4830

Richard A. Bourne Co., Inc., Box 141, Corporation St., Hyannis Port, MA 02647; (508) 775-0797

Robert C. Eldred Co., 1483 Route 6A, Box 796, East Dennis, MA 02641; (508) 385-3116

Selkirk's, 4166 Olive St., St. Louis, MO 63108; (314) 533-1700

Skinner, Inc., 2 Newbury St., Boston, MA 02116; (617) 236-1700

Sotheby's, 1334 York Ave., New York, NY 10021; (212) 606-7000

Texas Art Gallery, 1400 Main St., Dallas, TX 75202; (214) 747-8158

William Doyle Galleries, 175 East 87th St., New York, NY 10128; (212) 427-2730

Wolf's, 1239 West Sixth St., Cleveland, OH 44113; (216) 575-9653

4: American Appraiser Associations

American Society of Appraisers
Box 17265
Washington, DC 20041
(703) 478-2228

Antique Appraisers Association of America
11361 Garden Grove Blvd.
Garden Grove, CA 92643
(714) 530-7090

Appraisers Association of America
60 East 42nd St.
New York, NY 10165
(212) 867-9775

International Society of Fine Arts Appraisers
Box 280
River Forest, IL 60305
(312) 848-3340

New England Appraisers Association
5 Gill Terrace
Ludlow, VT 05149
(802) 228-7444
        or
104 Charles St.
Boston, MA 02114
(617) 523-6272

United States Appraisers Association, Inc.
1041 Tower Rd.
Winnetka, IL 60093
(312) 446-3434

5: Major American Art Dealer Associations

Art and Antique Dealers League of America
   353 East 78th St.
   Suite 19A
   New York, NY 10021
   (212) 879-7558

Art Dealers Association of America
   575 Madison Ave.
   New York, NY 10022
   (212) 940-8590

National Antique and Art Dealers Association of America
   15 East 57th St.
   New York, NY 10022
   (212) 826-9707

6: Art Reference Booksellers

Apollo Book
    5 Schoolhouse Lane
    Poughkeepsie, NY 12603
    To order a complimentary catalogue, call toll-free (800) 942-8222 (New York
        State residents only) or (800) 431-5003 (outside New York State).
Dealer's Choice
    Box 710
    Land O'Lakes, FL 34639
    To order a complimentary catalogue, call (813) 996-6599.
Hacker Art Books, Inc.
    54 West 57th Street
    New York, NY 10019
    To order a complimentary catalogue, call (212) 757-1450.
Hennessey + Ingalls Inc.
    1254 Santa Monica Mall
    Santa Monica, CA 90401
    (213) 458-9074

Index

Advertisements, 37–38
Affordability of art, 19–20
Altering art, 118
American appraiser associations, 197
American art dealer associations, major, 198
American auction houses, significant, 150, 196
American Institute for Conservation of Historic and Artistic Works, 113
Annuals, artist, 81, 193–194
Appraiser associations, American, 197
Archives, art, 81
Art. See also Buying art; Identifying art; Researching art; Selecting art
   academic side of, 26
   altering, 118
   archives, 81
   brochures about, 13
   business, 26–27, 43
   caring for, 117–118
   cleaning, 118
   as commodity, 135
   contemporary, 111
   display of, in galleries, 54
   dollar values of, 1
   economics of, 135–140
   emotional reactions to, 29–30
   established resources for, 36–37
   evaluating, 92–93, 99
   expense of, 1
   facts about, 28–29
   foreign, 38
   framing, 118
   inspecting condition of, 116–117
   as investment, 133, 138–139
   liquidity of, 136–137
   literature about, 13
   looking at, 12–14
   maintaining, 117–118
   market information on, 30

   money and, 133, 136
   offbeat resources for, 36–37
   older, 111
   original, 129
   paying for, 165–166
   "perfect," 36
   places of, 12
   preconceived notions about, 11
   price of, 97, 137
   protecting, 117
   quality of, 97
   raw feelings about, 11
   recording data on, 17–18
   repairing, 118
   restoring, 112–114
   temperature and, 117
   treating, 118
   types of, 12
   "uniqueness myth" of, 35–36
   unsigned, 126
   value of, 139–140
Artificial increases in value, 139–140
Artist annuals, 81, 193–194
Artist dictionaries, 80, 192–193
Artist directories, 81, 193–194
Artist encyclopedias, 80, 191
Artist indexes, 79–80, 190–191
Artists
   age of, 84
   awards received by, 85
   buying art for wrong reasons and, 11
   credentials of, 77
   dead, 105
   education of, 84
   European, 80
   exhibitions of, 85
   forgers and forgeries and, 122
   information about, 77–79
   organizational memberships of, 84–85
   price results on, 85
   private collections owning works by, 85

Artists, *continued*
  provenance and, 102
  public corporate collections owning
      works by, 85
  researching
      assessing facts in, 84–86
      biographical data on, 79–82
      example situations of, 86–89
      failure in, 86
      interpreting data on, 83–84
  signatures of, 124–127
The Art of the Forger, 124
Art piece. *See also* Art
  actual work vs. reproduction, 93
  file on, 167–168
  history of, 105
  major vs. minor work, 93–95
  originality of, 96–97
  owners of, 105–106
  price, 97
  provenance and, 102
  researching
      actual work vs. reproduction, 93
      date of, 96
      evaluating art and, 92–93, 99
      example situations of, 97–99
      faulty beliefs about, 91–92
      importance of, 91
      major vs. minor work, 93–95
      originality of, 96–97
      quality of, 97
      typical vs atypical work, 95–96
Atypical work, 95–96
Auction catalogues, 144–145
Auction houses, significant American, 150,
      196
Auction record compendiums, 144–146,
      147
Auction records, 81, 194–195
Auctions
  bidders at, 180–181
  buying art at, 175–178, 183–185
  description of, 175
  example situations of, 185–186
  forgers and forgeries and, 123
  galleries vs., 176–178
  liquidity of art and, 136–137
  misconceptions about, common,
      178–179
  as offbeat resources for art, 37

  plus points of, 181–182
  prices and, 142, 143–146
  return and exchange arrangements at,
      177
  value of work and, 146–151
Availability of art, 20

Bargaining. *See* Negotiating purchases
Benezit, 80
Bidders, 180–181
Biographical data on artists
  annuals, 81, 193–194
  archives, 81
  auction records, 81, 194–195
  dictionaries, 80, 192–193
  directories, 81, 193–194
  encyclopedias, 191
  files, 81
  indexes, 79–80, 190–191
  pointers on, 81–82
  price guides, 81, 194–195
Books, art, 57, 82
Booksellers, art reference, 199
Brochures, art, 13
Budget for buying art, 19–20
Business, art, 26–27, 43
Buyers, 14
Buying art
  artist's credentials and, 77
  at auctions, 175–178, 183–185
  budget for, 19–20
  constraints limiting, 21
  dont's of, 67–70
  economics of art and, 135–140
  example situations of, 70–72
  at galleries, 176–178
  general rules for, 19
  less-than-ideal conditions in, 171–172
  negotiating and
      advanced, 161–163
      dealers and, 162
      dos and don'ts of, 159–161
      procedure of, 158
      purpose of, 157
      relationship in, evolvement of,
          158–159
  from particular person, 21
  in past, 1
  people, 5

Buying art, *continued*
  in present, 1–2
  prices and
    auctions and, 142, 143–146
    dealers and, 141
    evaluating, 141–142
    galleries and, 142
    guides and, 153–155
    no-conflict-of-interest resources and,
      142, 151–153
    sellers, and, 142–143
    truth about, 141
  process of
    documenting, 166–168
    example situations of, 172–173
    less-than-ideal, 171–172
    paying, 165–166
    return and exchange arrangements in,
      168–171
  questions concerning, 2
  reasons for, 20
  from single gallery, 21
  situations of, 1–2
  wrong reasons for, 14

Caring for art, 117–118
Certificate of Authenticity, 166
Chemical detection of forgery, 128
Cleaning art, 118
Collecting and Care of Fine Arts, 117
Collecting art, 121. *See also* Buying art
Collectors, art, 27–28, 135
Comparison shopping
  contacting galleries for, 39–40
  established resources for, 36–37
  example situations of, 40–41
  locating galleries for, 37–38
  need for, 35
  offbeat resources for, 36–37
  preferences and, 36
  purpose of, 40
  reasons not to, 35–36
Condition Report, 116, 117, 166–167
Conservators, fine-art, 113–114, 118
Consignment arrangements, 169–170
Contemporary art, 111
Curators, museum, 26, 29–30, 139
Customers. *See* Dealer-customer
  relationship

Damaged art
  acceptable, 114–115
  contemporary art and, 111–112
  dealers and, 111, 115
  example situations of, 118–120
  galleries and, 111
  inspecting condition of art piece and,
    116–117
  location of damage and, 115
  maintaining art piece and, 117–118
  older works and, 111
  percentage of damage and, 115
  types of, 112–114
  value and, 112, 115
Dealer associations, major American, 198
Dealer-customer relationship
  example situations of, 64–65
  obligations in, 61
Dealer organizations, 38
Dealers. *See also* Dealer-customer
    relationship
  auction catalogues and, 144
  buying art for wrong reasons and, 11
  damaged art and, 111, 115
  dislikes of, 63–64
  economics of art and, 135
  likes of, 61–63
  negotiating and, 162
  organizations of, 38
  prices and, 141
  provenance and, 106
  selecting art
    caution regarding, 43–44
    characteristics of bad, 47–50
    characteristics of good, 46–47
    example situations of, 50–51
    truth about, 43
    usefulness of, 44–46
  speaking to, 28
  using emotional reactions, 47
Dictionaries, artist, 80, 192–193
Directories, artist, 81, 193–194
Documenting purchases, 166–168
Dollar values, 1. *See also* Prices
Dryness, 117

Economics of art
  aspects of, unique, 137–138
  collectors and, 135
  dealers and, 135

Economics of art, *continued*
  investment of art and, 138–139
  liquidity of art and, 136–137
  truths about, 135
  value of art and, 139–140
Emotional reactions, 29–30, 47
Encyclopedias, artist, 80, 191
Estate sales, 37
European artists, 80
Evaluating art, 92–93, 99
Exchange arrangements. *See* Return and
    exchange arrangements
Exhibition catalogues, 57, 82

Facts, 28–29
Fakes. *See* Forgers and forgeries
Files, art, 81, 167–168
Fine-art conservators, 113–114, 118
Flea markets, 37
Foreign art, 38
The Forger's Art, 124
Forgers and forgeries
  artists and, 122
  auctions and, 123
  dealers and, 121, 124, 126
  detecting, 123–124
  example situations of, 130–131
  in limited edition prints, 128–129
  methods for checking for, 127–128
  in sculptures, 129–130
  selling methods of, 122–123
  signatures and, 124–127
  verbal, 127
Framing art, 118

Galleries
  advertisements, 38
  art selected by, 35
  auctions vs., 176–178
  buying art at, 176–178
  buying art from single, 21
  contacting for selecting art, 39–41
  damaged art and, 111
  established, 36–37
  libraries of, 56–57
  locating for selecting art, 37–38
  long-term return/exchange arrangement,
    169
  preferences at, 37–38
  prices and, 142

  provenance and, 102
  quality at, 176
  return and exchange arrangements of,
    168–171, 177
  selecting art and
    back rooms of, 55–56
    design of, 53
    display of art in, 54
    example situations of, 58–59
    interiors of, 54–55
    meeting inside, 53
    offices of, 55–56
    storage areas of, 55–56
    "taking art home on approval"
      courtesy, 55, 168
    term of, 53
    tips on selecting, 57–58
    viewing conditions in, 54
  short-term return privilege, 169
  specialized, 176
  working list of, 39
Guarantee of Authenticity, 166

Humidity, effect on paintings, 117

Identifying art
  defining likes and
    being realistic about, 19–20
    being thorough about, 20–21
    recording data on, 17–18
  example situations of, 14–15
  looking at art and, 12–14
  raw feelings about, 11
  step of, 8
Indexes, artist, 79–80, 190–191
Infrared reflectometry, 127–128
Ink drawings, 125
Inspecting condition of art, 116–117
Installment payments, 166
International Directory of Arts, 38
International Foundation for Art Research
    (IFAR), 124
Investment, 133, 138–139

Libraries, art gallery, 56–57
Likes. *See* Preferences
Limited edition prints, forged, 128–129
Liquidation, art, 37
Liquidity of art, 136–137
Literature, art, 13

Long-term return/exchange arrangement, 169
Looking at art, 12–14

Magazines, art, 37–38, 57, 189
Maintaining art, 117–118
Major work, 93–95
Market information, 30
Microcracks, 128
Microscope, pocket, 128
Microscopy, polarizing, 128
Minor work, 93–95
Money. *See also* Prices
  art and, 133, 136
  dealers and, 48–49
Monographs, 82
Museum curators, 26, 29–30, 139

Negotiating purchases
  advanced, 161–163
  dealers and, 162
  dos and don'ts in, 159–161
  procedure of, 157–158
  purpose of, 157
  relationship in, evolvement of, 158–159
Newspapers, art, 37–38
Newspapers, local, 38
No-conflict-of-interest resources, 142, 151–153

Older art, 111
Original art, 129
Originality, 96
Owners of art piece, 105–106

Paying for art, 165–166
Pencil drawings, 125
Periodicals, art, 37–38, 57, 189
Photographic reproductions, 93, 129
Pigment identification, 128
Pocket microscope, 128
Polarizing microscopy, 128
Posthumous casting, 129
Preferences
  in beginning, 20
  being realistic about, 19–20
  being thorough about, 20–21
  comparison shopping and, 36
  galleries selling, 37–38
  recording data on, 17–18

Price guides. *See also* Prices
  artist's biographical data in, 81, 194–195
  in gallery libraries, 57
  list of, 194–195
  prices and, 153–155
Prices. *See also* Price guides
  art and, 97, 137
  art piece and, 97
  buying art and
    auctions and, 142, 143–146
    dealers and, 141
    evaluating, 141–142
    galleries and, 142
    guides and, 153–155
    no-conflict-of-interest resources and, 142, 151–153
    sellers and, 142–143
    truth about, 141
  fluctuations of, 135
  regulations for, 137
Price talk, 47–48
Proof of purchase, 166
Protecting art, 117
Provenance
  acquiring, 105–109
  artists and, 102
  art piece and, 102
  dealers and, 106
  definition of, 101
  example situations of, 107–109
  examples of, 101–102
  galleries and, 102
  hypothetical, 102–104
  maintaining, 105–109
  questions to ask in, 106–107
Purchases. *See also* Buying art
  documenting, 166–168
  future of, 165
  negative outcomes of, 165
  negotiating
    advanced, 161–163
    dealers and, 162
    dos and don'ts in, 159–161
    procedure of, 158
    purpose of, 157
    relationship in, evolvement of, 158–159
  process of
    documenting, 166–168

Purchases, process of, *continued*
example situations of, 172–173
less-than-ideal, 171–172
paying, 165–166
return and exchange arrangements in,
168–171

Quality, 97, 176

Real increases in value, 139–140
Receipt, 166
Reference sources, art, *See also* specific
types of
art annuals, 193–194
art directories, 193–194
artist dictionaries, 192–193
artist encyclopedias, 191
artist indexes, 190–191
auction records, 194–195
in gallery libraries, 56–57
price guides, 194–195
Referrals, 38
Repairing art, 118
Repeats, 97
Reproductions, 93, 129
Researching art
artists and
assessing facts in, 84–86
biographical data on, 79–82
example situations of, 86–89
failure in, 86
interpreting data from, 83–84
art piece and
actual work vs. reproduction, 93
date of, 96
evaluating art and, 92–93, 99
example situations of, 97–99
faulty beliefs and, 91–92
importance of, 91
major vs. minor work, 93–95
originality of, 96–97
quality of, 97
typical vs. atypical work, 95–96
damaged art and
acceptable damage, 114–115
contemporary art and, 111–112
dealers and, 111, 115
example situations of, 118–120
galleries and, 111

inspecting condition of art piece and,
116–117
location of damage, 115
maintaining art piece and, 117–118
older works and, 111
percentage of damage, 115
types of, 112–114
value and, 112, 115
forgers and forgeries and
artists and, 122
auctions and, 123
concern of, 121–122
dealers and, 121, 124, 126
detecting, 123–124
example situations of, 130–131
in limited edition prints, 128–129
methods for checking for, 127–128
in sculptures, 129–130
selling methods of, 122–123
signatures and, 124–127
truths about, 122
verbal, 127
learning about, 75
need for, 75
provenance and
acquiring, 105–109
artists and, 102
art piece and, 102
dealers and, 106
definition of, 101
example situations of, 107–109
examples of, 101–102
galleries and, 102
hypothetical, 102–104
maintaining, 105–107
questions to ask in, 106–107
rewards of, 75–76
step of, 8
Restoring art, 112–114
Return and exchange arrangements,
168–171, 177

Scholars, art, 26
Sculptures, forged, 129–130
Selecting art
comparison shopping and
contacting galleries for, 39–40
established resources for, 36–37
example situations of, 40–41

Selecting art, comparison shopping and,
continued
    locating galleries for, 37–38
    need for, 35
    offbeat resources for, 36–37
    preferences and, 36
    purpose of, 40
    reasons not to, 35–36
  dealer-customer relationship and,
    61–65
  dealers and
    caution regarding, 43–44
    characteristics of bad, 47–50
    characteristics of good, 46–47
    example situations of, 50–51
    truth about, 43
    usefulness of, 44–46
  don'ts of buying art and, 67–70
  galleries and
    back rooms of, 55–56
    design of, 53
    display of art in, 54
    example situations of, 58–59
    interiors of, 54–55
    libraries of, 56–57
    meeting in, 53
    offices of, 55–56
    storage areas of, 55–56
    "taking art home on approval"
      courtesy of, 55
    term of, 53
    tips on selecting, 57–58
    viewing conditions in, 54
  people involved in, speaking to
    example situations of, 32–33
    how to take what they say, 30–32
    lessons learned from, 25–26
    what they say, 28–30
    who they are, 26–28
Sellers
  Condition Report and, 116, 117
  false beliefs of, 45
  of forgeries, 122–123
  prices and, 142–143
  speaking to, 26–27

Shopping. *See* Comparison shopping
Short-term return privilege, 169
Signatures, 124–127
Solubility tests, 128
Sunlight, 117

"Taking art home on approval" courtesy,
    55, 169
Temperature, 117
Theime-Becker, 80
Theime-Becker's supplement, 80
Treating art, 118
Typical work, 95–96

Ultraviolet light, 127
Unconditional Money-Back Guarantee,
    167
"Uniqueness myth," 35–36
Unsigned art, 126

Value
  of art, 139–140
  artificial increases in, 139–140
  auctions and, 146–151
  economics of art and, 139–140
  real increases in, 139–140
Verbal forgeries, 127
Viewing room, 54
Vollmer, 80

"Water crayons," 111
Work of art. *See* Art; Art piece

Yard sales, 37
Yellow Pages, 38